T
James E

LHP

Also by Thomas D. Perry

Ascent To Glory: The Genealogy of J. E. B. Stuart

God's Will Be Done: The Christian Life of J. E. B. Stuart

The Dear Old Hills Of Patrick:" J. E. B. Stuart and Patrick County Virginia

"Whatever May Be My Fate, May You Be Happy." J. E. B. Stuart, Bettie Hairston and the Beaver Creek Plantation

The Free State of Patrick: Patrick County Virginia in the Civil War

Never Forget: Martinsville, Patrick and Henry Counties in Vietnam

"If Thee Must Fight, Fight Well" William J. Palmer and the Battle of Martinsville Virginia April 8, 1865

The Graham Mansion: A History

Fieldale Virginia

Martinsville Virginia

Ararat Virginia: A Guide From Willis Gap to Kibler Valley

Mount Airy North Carolina

Beyond Mayberry: A Memoir of Andy Griffith and Mount Airy North Carolina

Notes From the Free State of Patrick: Patrick County, Virginia, and Regional History

Patrick County Oral History Project: A Guide

www.freestateofpatrick.com

The Papers of James Ewell Brown Stuart

Volume One 1833-1854
Son of Southwest Virginia

Edited by Thomas D. Perry

Copyright 2017 Thomas David Perry. All rights reserved.

ISBN-13: 978-1479257034

ISBN-10: 1479257036

 Laurel Hill Publishing
www.freestateofpatrick.com

Thomas D. "Tom" Perry
4443 Ararat Highway
P O Box 11
Ararat VA 24053

276-692-5300
freestateofpatrick@yahoo.com
www.freestateofpatrick.com

"I cannot recognize General Stuart's fame as being the exclusive property of anyone."
-- John S. Mosby

For James I. "Bud" Robertson, Jr.

Teacher, Friend, and Mentor

The first known picture of James Ewell Brown "Jeb" Stuart believed to be during his first year at the United States Military Academy at West Point, New York, circa 1850.

Table of Contents

Volume One: The Making of a Soldier:
February 1833-September 1854
11

Listing of Individual Letters
13

Chapter One: Son of Southwest Virginia:
February 1833-June 1850
15

Chapter Two: The Education of a Solider:
July 1850-September 1854
31

Index
133

About the Author
137

J. E. B. Stuart during the War Between the States (1861-64).

Volume One: The Making of a Soldier: February 1833-September 1854

I cannot remember when James Ewell Brown "Jeb" Stuart was not part of my life. As a child growing up in Ararat, Patrick County, Virginia, Stuart was on the bank sign about a mile north of my home on Route 773, the Ararat Highway. His birthplace was noted by a Virginia Historical Highway Marker, two miles south on the same road. We did not have road names then in the 1960s. Today, the Ararat Highway takes residents and a few visitors to the site I worked to save in the late 1990s.

For many years, I collected Stuart's letters, reports, and any papers to hopefully one day present them together into a book, which I now project as a three-volume work on the life of a man, who only lived thirty-one years.

James Ewell Brown "Jeb" Stuart was born on February 6, 1833, to Archibald and Elizabeth Letcher Pannill Stuart at the Laurel Hill Farm in what is today Ararat, Virginia. The Patrick County seat named for Stuart is over twenty-five miles away. There is no evidence that he ever set foot in the town that bears his name today.

This first volume covers Stuart's first twenty-one years of life including his time going to school in Wythe and Pulaski Counties in Southwest Virginia, and a nearly two-year stint at Emory and Henry College. Stuart then went to the United States Military Academy at West Point, New York. This book covers those events in his life. The second volume will cover Stuart's time in the United States Army from 1854 until 1861, mainly in the First United States Cavalry in Kansas Territory, but also in the Regiment of Mounted Rifles in Texas. The third volume will cover Stuart's time in the service of the Confederate States of America rising to the rank of Major General commanding the cavalry of Robert E. Lee's Army of Northern Virginia.

It is my hope that my years of research on Stuart will give the readers a thorough background on the man and his history surrounding his role in the history of the United and Confederate States of America.

Tom Perry, July 2017, Ararat, Virginia

The original Virginia Historical Highway Marker placed in December 1932 at the Laurel Hill Farm (J. E. B. Stuart's Birthplace) in Ararat, Virginia. Historian Douglas S. Freeman is believed to have been the editor of the sign. In 2001, this author wrote the text for the new marker placed at the site and the original is now in possession of the editor.

Listing of Individual Letters

To	Date	J. E. B. Stuart's Location	Location
Chapter One			
Alexander Stuart Brown	4/11/1846	Wytheville, VA	VHS
Elizabeth Letcher Pannill Stuart	12/6/1846	Wytheville, VA	VHS
Alexander Stuart Brown	1/17/1847	Draper's Valley, VA	VHS
Alexander Stuart Brown	undated circa 1857	Wytheville, VA	VHS
Alexander Stuart Brown	3/25/1848	Wytheville, VA	VHS
Peregrine Buckingham	9/4/1849	Emory and Henry College	MoC
George W. Crawford	4/8/1850	Patrick County, VA	DNA
Alexander Stuart Brown	6/3/1850	Washington, DC	MoC
Chapter Two			
Alexander Stuart Brown	7/8/1850	West Point, NY	VHS
George Hairston	8/17/1850	West Point, NY	VHS
Alexander Stuart Brown	10/21/1850	West Point, NY	VHS
Alexander Stuart Brown	10/25/1850	West Point, NY	VHS
Alexander Stuart Brown	1/24/1851	West Point, NY	VHS
George Hairston	3/6/1851	West Point, NY	VHS
Archibald Stuart	3/25/1851	West Point, NY	VHS
Archibald Stuart	6/2/1851	West Point, NY	COCG
Archibald Stuart	7/22/1851	West Point, NY	VHS
George Hairston	8/13/1851	West Point, NY	VHS
Alexander Stuart Brown	12/13/1851	West Point, NY	VHS
George Hairston	12/25/1851	West Point, NY	VHS
George Hairston	4/13/1852	West Point, NY	VHS
Alexander Stuart Brown	4/20/1852	West Point, NY	VHS
Archibald Stuart	5/21/1852	West Point, NY	COCG
Elizabeth Letcher Pannill Stuart	9/1/1852	West Point, NY	USMA
Bettie Hairston	9/23/1852	West Point, NY	UNC
Bettie Hairston	11/6/1852	West Point, NY	UNC
Bettie Hairston	12/20/1852	West Point, NY	UNC
Helen Alexander	1/6/1853	West Point, NY	MoC
Bettie Hairston	3/23/1853	West Point, NY	UNC
Archibald Stuart	4/5/1853	West Point, NY	COCG
Bettie Hairston	5/17/1853	West Point, NY	UNC
Alexander Hugh Holmes Stuart	5/30/1853	West Point, NY	Private
Bettie Hairston	6/29/1853	West Point, NY	UNC
Bettie Hairston	8/17/1853	West Point, NY	UNC
Bettie Hairston	10/28/1853	West Point, NY	UNC
Archibald Stuart	circa 1854	West Point, NY	McCl
Bettie Hairston	2/9/1854	West Point, NY	UNC
Bettie Hairston	5/8/1854	West Point, NY	UNC
Mrs. Claudius Beard	6/9/1854	Washington, DC	MoC
Peter Hairston	8/3/1854	Salem, NC	UNC

Listing of Individual Letters

To	Date	J. E. B. Stuart's Location	Location
Prayer	9/10/1854		Private
Bettie Hairston	9/27/1854	Richmond/Salem, VA	UNC
Poem To Bettie	12/24/1853	West Point, NY	UNC

Key To Locations Holding Stuart Papers

COCG	Occidental College, California
DNA	National Archives, Washington D. C.
McCL	I Rode With J. E. B. Stuart by H. B. McClellan
MoC	Museum of the Confederacy, Richmond, Virginia
Poetry	J. E. B. Stuart Poetry Album
VHS	Virginia Historical Society, Richmond, Virginia
VSL	Virginia State Library, Richmond, Virginia
UNC	University of North Carolina at Chapel Hill, North Carolina
USMA	United States Military Academy, West Point, New York
Private	Personal Collections of Anonymous Individuals

CHAPTER ONE

Son of Southwest Virginia

February 6, 1833-June 3, 1850

TO ALEXANDER STUART BROWN[1]

Wytheville, Virginia[2]

April 11, 1846

My Dear Cousin,

I received your letter yesterday and was glad to hear that you were so well pleased with Emory and Henry.[3] I believe there is no news about Wytheville worth your attention. We are all well here except Sukey[4] who has the measles. I have also had them since I have been here. I like your college very well only I could not do without butter. I was very much pleased with your amusements. I am very much pleased with Wytheville so far. Contrary to the expectations of all I have been so fortunate as not to have a single fight since I have been going to school not from cowardice either (for I know you will immediately suspect that as being the reason) but it was by forming a firm resolution never to be imposed upon. If they saw immediately so far from trying to do it they acted quite to the contrary.

As to Madam Phoebe's (I will not call her Miss because she has passed that title) colt I think it will undoubtedly be a sorrel for it has been adding more and more to that colour ever since its birth. As to that gender—it is of the masculine which I expect is very pleasant news to you. Lee is not here now but I will see him tonight and add his account in

---

[1] Alexander Stuart Brown (1831-1859) was the son of Judge James Ewell Brown and Anne Dabney Stuart, uncle and aunt of J. E. B. Stuart.
[2] Wytheville in Wythe County, Virginia, named for George Wythe.
[3] Emory and Henry College near Abingdon, Virginia, was founded in 1836 and named for Methodist Bishop John Henry.
[4] Sukey was a slave from Laurel Hill, the birthplace of J. E. B. Stuart.

the Post Script, vacation I expect to go home. Pa[5] is here at this time and will leave here next Monday. He sends his love to John and you. Tell John that I want him to fulfill his promise. Rose is in fine order and as gaily as need for. Tell John Dabney Stuart[6] that when Pa came home he concluded he would try my rifle and the cap being off he took it for granted that it was not loaded and put another bullet down and came very near shooting it off before he found it out. Give my love to John Dabney Stuart and excuse this abominable letter and believe me.

Your affectionate cousin,

    J. E. B. Stuart

P. S. Lee says your chickens are coming on very well and says your favorite hen was killed by a pole cat. He has two wild cats setting which will hatch next week. He says your cock which you gave to Mr. Baily is still here and fights manly. – J. E. B. S.

TO ELIZABETH LETCHER PANNILL STUART[7]

    Cobbler Spring[8], December 6, 1846

My Dear Mother,

    I took it upon myself to borrow a horse and come up here, being Sunday, and here I found Uncle Jack who expects to start for home tomorrow and I thought I would take advantage of this opportunity to write to you, although I must confess my conscience is in opposition

---

[5] Archibald Stuart (1795-1855), father of J. E. B. Stuart, served in both houses of Virginia legislature, two constitutional conventions for Virginia (1829-30, 1850-1851) and one term in United States House of Representatives (1837-1839).
[6] Dr. John Dabney Stuart (1828-1877), brother of J. E. B. Stuart, practiced medicine in Floyd County before, as a surgeon in the Fifty-Fourth Virginia Infantry Regiment during and in Wythe County after the Civil War.
[7] Elizabeth Letcher Pannill Stuart (1801-1884) was the mother of J.E.B. Stuart.
[8] Home of Judge James Ewell Brown (1789-1852), uncle and man J. E. B. Stuart is named, located on Pepper's Ferry Road in Wythe County, Virginia.

with my pen for I can't tell why you don't write to me, for you have no idea how acceptable a letter from home is of any sort, especially to me away off at boarding school where I never hear from home or anywhere else. I have no doubt that you have all experience this, and for that reason it appears still more astonishing why you do not have mercy on a poor little insignificant whelp away from his mammy. I hope you will not defer writing any longer, but WRITE! WRITE! WRITE!

I saw Brother Alex[9] in town today—he was well. I know by this time you are impatient to know something about Mr. Painter's[10]. All I have to say is simply this, that it is a first rate place, but I had rather go to Mr. Buchanan[11].

Tell Vic[12] that I have gotten arithmetic for her—and it is a very pretty one, and if I had any idea of Uncle Jack's being here I would have brought it up. Kiss her for me and also Dave. I would also tell you to kiss Bellors and Dollors, but I know you would not do that. Give my love to Papa, sisters Mary and Columbia and Victoria[13]. Give my best regards to Mr. Ayers[14] when you see him. I wrote a long letter to him yesterday.

    I ever remain

    Your affectionate son,

    J. E. B. Stuart

---

[9] William Alexander Stuart (1826-1892), brother of J. E. B. Stuart, Clerk of Court in Wythe County, Virginia before the Civil War, operated salt works in Saltville, Virginia, during the war, and was a cattle and businessman after the war.

[10] Dr. George Whitfield Painter, minister in Draper Valley, Pulaski County, Virginia, who operated a boarding school for boys in his home Hillcrest.

[11] Attorney Peregrine Buchanan operated a boy's school in Wytheville, Virginia

[12] Victoria Augusta Stuart, sister of J. E. B. Stuart, married N. A. Boyden of North Carolina.

[13] Mary Tucker Stuart (1821-1888), Columbia Lafayette Stuart (1830-1857), and Victoria Augusta Stuart were sisters of J. E. B. Stuart

[14] Parris Ayres (Ayers) was a merchant in Patrick County, Virginia.

P.S. I deemed it unnecessary to say in this that I was well for you know I am never anything else–J. E. B. S.

TO ALEXANDER STUART BROWN

Draper's Valley, Virginia, January 17, 1847

It is now dear cousin almost a month since I wrote to you last and I resume my seat hoping that you will—

View this not with a scornful eye

But pass its imperfections by

Although I have but little new to write yet I hope that I will have something that will interest you.

I was disappointed in getting a horse here. So I set out on foot on Tuesday[15] morning for Uncle Brown's. I crossed the mountain and went up the back road by Graham's[16], where I dined upon quite a fine dinner, and then set out on my journey the snow being about half leg deep and I tell you that I had a tough time of it, for I had to break the road nearly all the way.

I got to Cobbler Springs about sundown where I found Cousins T. and F., also Miss Mary McKee and Miss Maria S. Crockett who was as fat and pretty as ever. I had the pleasure of riding home with her next morning and in the conversation I brought up your name, and I talked about a good many different things concerning you and found them to be o. k. but away with this trash.

When I got there I found that I could not get a horse (I mean at Uncle Brown's) until he arrived home which he did not until Thursday night following. I thought it was not worth my while to go to Patrick County[17] until spring at which time I intend to go or burst a gut.

---

[15] December 22, 1847.
[16] Major David Graham's mansion, Max Meadows, Wythe County, Virginia.
[17] Laurel Hill, the birthplace and boyhood home of J. E. B. Stuart is located in

I stayed there enjoying myself most remarkably well, until Tuesday[18] making a stay of just two weeks when accompanied with Miss Maria Young I came down to the Valley where I have been ever since jogging away at old Caesar.

I suppose you've heard of the wedding etc. The Colonel[19] has gone with a carriage to Roanoke after his children. Things are going on about as usual. I received a letter from Sister Columbia the other day. They were all well and she requested me to send her love to you when I wrote to you. My school will be out the last of March. I want to go home then and stay until May and then go to Mr. Buckingham.

Yours,

J. E. B. Stuart

TO ALEXANDER STUART BROWN

Wytheville, Virginia, Undated circa 1847

Dear Cousin,

I received your most affectionate letter in due time and have delayed the answer so that I might write something about the wedding but I reckon your other correspondents have already written enough to make you tired of the business. I therefore will not go into detail of the affair, but just skip about and touch on various heads. The first thing which I suppose will occupy your mind will be Miss Maria Crockett[20]. She was there I say, that lovely creature was there in all her beauty and would that you had been there. Nothing would have pleased me more

---

Ararat, Patrick County, Virginia.

[18] January 5, 1847.

[19] Thomas J. Boyd (1804-1893) was an attorney and legislator from Wythe County, Virginia.

[20] Maria Crockett Gleaves (1829-1878) was the daughter of Charles and Mary H. Crockett and brother of Lucian Crockett. She married Dr. Samuel C. Gleaves (1823-1890).

than to have seen you and your lovely Maria seated together. I reckon you can imagine your own happiness on the occasion if you had been there. At the wedding there were but few. All that were there (except one or two) were relations. I believe Miss Maria Crockett carried the day (or rather the night). Brother Alex I think did his best but I think he came out at the little end of the horn but I do not know. You must take all I say merely as my own private opinion. Neither was Mr. Buckingham behind hand but he and Old Charley occupied a good deal of this time in talking over political affairs. Upon the whole I think that they all enjoyed themselves very much. Miss Maria Young and Miss Nannie Richardson[21] were also there. Gordon Kent[22] seemed to pay the most attention to them at the party. Things went on about the same.

I am still going to school to Mr. Buckingham and boarding at Mr. Millers[23]. Your old sweetheart Miss M. Peirce[24] is there at this time. You are mistaken in thinking that I am in love with Virginia Miller[25] for nothing is farther from me and if it were not that I am boarding there I would tell you the reason there is not the least danger of my trespassing on holy ground. And another thing I have gotten out with the girls. I believe they were just made for man's troubles. There is no girl now that I care anything about except Miss Maria Crockett and I do not care a great deal "about" her.

I am determined to devote this Session to the hardest kind of study. I am still reading Caesar (in which I think I will be perfect at the end of this Session expiring last of July) and Algebra in which I have

---

[21] Nannie Richardson taught music at Wytheville Female College.
[22] Gordon C. Kent was a farmer and businessman in Wythe County, Virginia.
[23] James R. Miller operated the Bell Tavern in Wytheville, Virginia.
[24] Mary Belle Pierce was a niece of J. E. B. Stuart and daughter of James and Nancy Anne Dabney Stuart Pierce.
[25] Virginia Miller was the daughter of James R. Miller with whom J. E. B. Stuart boarded with in Wytheville, Virginia.

gotten as far as Evolution of Powers. I have some business to attend to so I must hasten and conclude. I will not say anything about that scrape at Mr. Painter's' but will leave it for your own inspection. Excuse this badly written letter and believe me your affectionate cousin, etc., etc., etc.

   J. E. B. Stuart

P. S. Write soon and you said you would send a note in your last letter to Miss Maria but you did not.

TO ALEXANDER STUART BROWN

   Wytheville, Virginia, March 25, 1848

My Dear Cousin,

  It has been a siege since I have either written to you or received a letter from you and since that time I have underwent a good deal of suffering. I suppose you have heard of the severe spell of sickness I had last fall, and even at this time my head is as bald as an eagle and I am very much laughed at by the gals.

  Although I have nothing to write back which would in the least interest you I thought I would write anyhow for the sake of reviving our old correspondence. And I assure you that a letter from such a fine polished gentleman as yourself can't help but be very acceptable to a youth of <u>14</u>. But <u>were I to consider my own reputation perhaps I should remain silent on this occasion</u>. But away with this nonsense I must try and write something which will be worth the five cents you have to pay for this.[26] After I recovered from the fever I went to Patrick County and stayed there until that sad disaster of having our house burnt (which I expect you have heard of) happened[27]. Then I came through

---

[26] Postal fees were paid by those receiving mail.
[27] The house Stuart was born in burned during the winter of 1847-48 at Laurel Hill.

Floyd County to this place. Ma and Vic[28] are in Floyd at this time where I expect they will spend the summer. Columbia[29] is in Pittsylvania. We have not decided whether we will build again or not. John Stuart[30] stayed with Dr. Headen[31] studying medicine until our house was burnt and then came home and he and Pa are now keeping house in the kitchen. John gets books from Dr. Headen by Pa every Floyd Court. Alick is at this time in Patrick County. After I came here I concluded I would work in the County Office with Alick[32] until about next August and then I am going to the College[33]. I heard tonight that Colonel William Byars[34] died on Monday last with Paralysis. I suppose he was an old friend of yours.

There is a singing school in town at this time taught by J. B. Wise. He has a great many scholars both male and female—among others I am a scholar. Mr. Wise has composed several pieces of music for the piano and you never heard the like of so much music. Mr. Wise some say is rather pleased with Miss Mary Miller[35] for he has gallanted her several times. But don't tell Mat this for I am afraid it will make him leave the College to see about it. I have not seen Miss Maria in town in a coon's age. I believe she has quit Louis all together. I suppose you of course have heard of the arrival of Miss Betsey Kent[36] who is very pretty indeed. Our kitchen caught fire the other night by Celia[37] going up stairs

---

[28] Victoria Stuart, sister of J. E. B. Stuart.
[29] Columbia L. Stuart, sister of J. E. B. Stuart.
[30] John Dabney Stuart, brother of J. E. B. Stuart.
[31] Dr. Tazewell Headen, husband of Mary Tucker Stuart, sister of J. E. B. Stuart, was a physician in Floyd County, Virginia.
[32] William Alexander Stuart, brother of J. E. B. Stuart.
[33] J. E. B. Stuart worked for his brother William Alexander Stuart in the clerk's office in Wythe County before enrolling into Emory and Henry College.
[34] Byars was the first President of Emory and Henry College Board of Trustees.
[35] Mary Miller was the daughter of Darius and Sarah Miller of Wythe County, Virginia.
[36] Ann Elizabeth Kent was the daughter of Robert Kent of Wythe County, Virginia. She later married John Dabney Stuart, brother of J. E. B. Stuart.
[37] Celia was a slave from Laurel Hill.

with her pipe. It is supposed a coal of fire must have dropped from it. It was put out before any harm was done. The Court House bell was rung 15 minutes, and I and Alick slept so soundly that we never heard it.

There is a great deal of excitement about the election of Virginia's delegate from this city. The following gents are candidates: Viz., Thomas J. Boyd, George Walton, James L. Yost, Thomas M. Smyth, Democrat and George Coon (but he looks more like an opossum)[38]. I think Colonel Boyd will be nominated by the caucus. Mr. Smyth has written a very able and lengthy circular. But I am afraid he will have to knock under. Now Cousin Alick I think this a right long letter considering I had none to answer and I shall expect just such a one in answer. I saw a copy of "The Wreath" which Mat sent to Alick and I was very much pleased with it for it will _____ the editors. With well wishes for your future welfare and happiness I remain your sincere friend and affectionate cousin.

James E. B. Stuart

Give my love to all your <u>friends</u>

For your friends are my friends.

TO MR. BUCKINGHAM

Emory and Henry College

September 4, 1849

Dear Sir,

As I am endeavoring to graduate in two years, I find that I will not have time to complete 6 books of the Aenead of Virgil required without taking on five studies for one Session which would be rather difficult to do. When I was under your supervision, you know I

---

[38] Thomas J. Boyd, George Walton, James L. Yost, Thomas M. Smyth, and George Coon were residents of Wythe County, Virginia.

commenced Virgil, but after a few weeks reading was taken sick and saw no more of my books until I came here. Since I have been here I have read Cicero and Livy, the former an equal and the latter a superior test of scholarship to Virgil, but still the Professor in that department does not seem willing to let me off from Virgil without something of the nature of a certificate from you. This therefore is my object in writing to you now. I wish you, if you feel justified in so doing, to send me a written certificate saying that though I did not read 6 books of the Aenead (Aeneid) still you believe my scholarship sufficient to enter advanced classes in Latin. Now I do not presume to think that my scholarship was at all sufficient in your estimation, or in that of any other accomplished linguist, but I wish you to bear in mind that proficiency with you and proficiency here are far different things. Taking the above into consideration I hope you will not hesitate to grant the favor I ask. I have already advanced in the course beyond Virgil.

Although I am deprived of your excellent instruction still I am trying to stick to the old principles of reading Latin which you instilled into me party by the mouth and partly by the <u>rod</u>. I am now reading Ovid, and I think it quite a treat to launch from the dry facts of Livy into the beauties of Ovid. It is not my intention not to read Virgil at all, but as I expect to teach school some when I leave here, then will be my time to read.

Your sincere friend in haste, J. E. B. Stuart

TO GEORGE W. CRAWFORD[39]

Patrick County, Virginia, April 8, 1850

Honorable George W. Crawford

The Secretary of War

---

[39] George W. Crawford (1796-1872) of Augusta, Georgia, was Secretary of War under President Franklin Pierce.

Washington City, D. C.

Sir:

I have the honor to acknowledge the receipt of your communication of the fifth ultimo informing me that the President had conferred upon me a conditional appointment of Cadet in the service of the United States, and to inform you of my acceptance of the same.

Yours respectfully, your obedient servant

James E. B. Stuart

I hereby assent to the above acceptance by my son of his conditional appointment as Cadet, and he has my full permission to sign articles by which we will bind himself to serve the United States eight years unless soon discharged.

Archibald Stuart

TO ALEXANDER STUART BROWN

Irving House, Washington, D. C., June 3, 1850

Dear Cousin,

For once, true to my promise I take pleasure in retiring to my room in order that I may give you some account of my trip thus far as well as my day's stay in "The Great Metropolis."

I would not have been worthy of the name of Stuart had I arrived here safely and without losing or forgetting something. This I knew but thought that a man was not obliged to lose the clothes off his back for the sake of inheriting a name. But such was the fact in my case. I lost my badge while riding on the driver's seat on the stage the day after I left Wytheville. In brushing some dust off my coat collar I touched it accidentally and the dust was an inch thick so that finding it was impossible. I dined that day with sister Bethenia[40]-all were well. I met

---

[40] Bethenia Stuart (1819-circa 1910), sister of J. E. B Stuart, married Nicholas

the California boys at Salem, Virginia. I arrived at Lynchburg the next evening where I stayed two days with Uncle Dabney Chiswell[41]. I was very much pleased with my Cousins Lucy and Kittie[42]-the latter especially-I had an idea what pretty cousins I had. They were a little reserved at first, but his soon disappeared and they treated me more as a brother than as a stranger. I had the pleasure too of becoming acquainted with Cousin George William Dabney[43]. Cousin Kittie says you must be sure to call on her on your way to Charlottesville. Take care you don't leave your heart in her custody-she plays and sings delightfully. One thing you will be struck with in her singing, that is, distinct articulation, with a sweet voice.

I left there for Charlottesville where I stayed one day. I went all over the University [of Virginia][44] and became acquainted with General Cabell[45] and his two sons from whom I received a letter of introduction to Cadet W. Lewis Cabell, [46]and Captain Witcher. Dick Sanders[47] and I went over to Monticello which is truly a romantic place. I have a small piece of the marble slab over his grave with this inscription: "Here was buried Thomas Jefferson, author of the Declaration of Independence, the statute of Virginia for religious freedom, and father of the University of Virginia." I pulled also two roses from near the walk leading through his

---

Chevalier.
[41] Chiswell Dabney (1791-1865) lived in Amherst County, Virginia, and was a distant relative of J. E. B. Stuart and Lady Astor.
[42] Lucy Dabney Otey and Elizabeth "Kittie" Dabney Langhorne were daughters of Chiswell Dabney.
[43] George William Dabney was a son of Chiswell Dabney.
[44] The University of Virginia founded by Thomas Jefferson in 1819.
[45] General Benjamin W. S. Cabell (1793-1862) served on staff of Major General John Pegram in the War of 1812.
[46] W. Lewis Cabell (1827-1911) was a graduate of the USMA Class of 1850 and a Confederate Brigadier General.
[47] Richard W. Sanders of Max Meadows, Virginia, was a student at the University of Virginia.

yard. There is a statue of him in front of the President's house here. It is made of bronze with the Declaration in his hand cut into bronze. The statue was presented during Tyler's Administration[48] to the President by the owner of Mr. Jefferson's residence, Captain Levy, United States Navy.[49] I went from Charlottesville to the junction where I left my overcoat and then came immediately on here.

You have no idea how delightful steamboat traveling is until you try it. I came here last evening and am as green as a gourd vine yet. Unfortunately I did not come on reception days (Tuesday and Friday) and was thereby deprived of the pleasure of an introduction to Zack [President Zachary Taylor]. I have seen him twice on the streets. He is a plain looking old fellow with a slight squat as he walks. I walked all around the White House and buildings and was also in the parlor but except on Tuesdays and Fridays [President] General Taylor rarely shows himself.[50]

I called on Dr. Averett[51] this morning whom I found a very fine sensible old gentleman indeed. I went up to the Capitol at an early hour- say 10 o'clock-and the Senators kept dropping in by degrees until 12 when the Vice President Millard Fillmore[52] came in and called the Senate to Order, and believe me when I say a day in the United States Senate is worth no little to anyone but especially to one who wishes to acquire a practical knowledge of parliamentary usages. The first thing done was

---

[48] John Tyler (1790-1862) was the Eleventh President of the United States.
[49] Uriah P. Levi (1792-1862) was a Commodore in U. S. Navy and owner of Monticello.
[50] Zachary Taylor (1784-1850) was the Twelfth President of the United States of America.
[51] Dr. Thomas Averett (1800-1855) succeeded Archibald Stuart as a member of the United States House of Representatives and appointed Stuart to the United States Military Academy at West Point, New York.
[52] Millard Fillmore (1800-1874) Vice-President under Zachary Taylor and became Thirteenth President of the United States of America on Taylor's death.

the reading by the secretary of a message from the President, enclosing a letter from some foreign minister and when Daniel Webster[53] asked what it was in reference to he read again, and it was about an improved breed of silk-worms, recommending their introduction into the United States. This you may know created laughter. I think Mr. Webster is decidedly the finest looking man in the Senate. He speaks slowly but forcibly, but of all pleasant speakers give me Jefferson Davis of Mississippi.[54] I hear Mr. Clay[55] make some remarks. He is very nervous and gesticulates, but his voice is clear and his countenance always wears an air of dignity and command which give him a noble appearance while speaking. He has a frankness of manner which adds much to his speaking. Mr. Fillmore is a better looking man than I expected to find him. Foote[56] puts me very much in mind of Abram Painter[57] of Cripple Creek. Mr. Samuel Houston[58] is very fine looking and I think that he appears better with his mouth shut than open. Walker[59] of Wisconsin is a good looking man. Young Clemens[60] of Alabama is really handsome and looks like a boy among men with his youthful countenance. You can always, at this time, tell a man of Congress by having crepe on his left arm in mourning for Senator Ellmore[61]. Messrs. Jefferson Davis of Mississippi and Douglas[62] of Illinois discussed the merits of the California question while I was in. Mr. Davis is hard to beat. Benton[63] made a speech in reference to

---

[53] Daniel Webster (1782-1852) was a Senator from Massachusetts.
[54] Jefferson Davis (1808-1889) was a Senator from Mississippi, Secretary of War under Franklin Pierce and President of the Confederate States of America.
[55] Henry Clay (1777-1852) was a Senator from Kentucky.
[56] Henry S. Foote (1804-1880) was a Senator from Mississippi.
[57] Abram Painter is listed in the 1850 Census of Wythe County, Virginia.
[58] Samuel Houston (1793-1863) was a Senator from Texas and a distant relative of J. E. B. Stuart through Letcher family.
[59] Issac Walker (1815-1872) was a Senator from Wisconsin.
[60] Jeremiah Clemens (1814-1865) was a Senator from Alabama.
[61] Franklin H. Ellmore (1799-1850) was a Senator from South Carolina.
[62] Stephen A. Douglas (1813-1861) was a Senator from Illinois.

something else-I don't admire this manner. Dawne[64] of Louisa is a miserable declaimer. Mr. Cass[65] is a fleshy old fellow with a very fat face and fat under the chin. He had nothing to say today.

I was in the House but this was a rowdy place compared with the Senate. I enclose you a plan of the Senate Chamber. I have marked the seats of those absent today with an asterisk. The lawn around the Capitol is a very pretty and pleasant place. I have a twig of an arbor vitae tree growing in it. There is a fountain in front of the Capitol around a monument erected to some officers who died in the War with Great Britain. On the cap stone of one pillar of the monument stands Hermes with a gilt wand in his hand. On another Pallas.

Excuse this scrawl and believe me your true friend and affectionate cousin [,] James.

Write immediately. I leave in the (train) cars for Baltimore at 5 in the morning.

P. S. My love to all-Tell Brother Alex my letter to him will be dated July 1st, 1850.

---

[63] Thomas H. Benton (1782-1858) was a Senator from Missouri.
[64] Solomon Downs (1801-1854) was a Senator from Louisiana.
[65] Lewis Cass (1782-1866) was a Senator from Michigan.

A photo of Archibald Stuart taken while serving in the Virginia Senate 1852-54. Courtesy of the Virginia Historical Society.

Chapter Two: The Education of a Soldier July 1850-September 1854

TO ALEXANDER STUART BROWN

    Camp Gaines, United States Military Academy,

    West Point, New York, July 8, 1850

My Dear Cousin

    Your highly interesting letter was received with great pleasure, and the flattering terms in which you spoke of my Washington letter, as well as the peculiar pleasure it ever affords me to correspond with friends, have induced me to try the game again, not however with the least hope that this scrawl will merit the encomiums you heaped upon the other.

    I was gratified to hear from your letter that you had laid aside old Coke for a while for the purpose of taking a little recreation on New River, satisfied as I am that no spot of Western Virginia can be better calculated to please interest and captivate the student. Major Taylor's mansion will ever bear associations to me of friendship and respect. I know the Major as well as if I had a formal introduction to him.

    You seem to think that cousin Kittie completely captured my heart, but although my description of her may have warranted such an inference, yet my heart is free, and true to my promise <u>made to her</u>, my object was to captivate <u>you</u> by the <u>description</u>; for be assured if I had really fallen in love with her, you would have been the last man to hear of her beauty from me as I know how formidable a rival you are when you take a notion.

    But of all the places to cure love give me West Point. I have not thought of such a thing as a sweetheart since I came to the Point, and yet I have thought more of friends and relatives than ever before in my life; it is a great place to wean one from home; in truth it is a great place in every respect, great for the facilities for education, as a finishing school for manners and refinement, for studying human nature, learning the ways of the world and for straightening the form, but more of this in its proper place.

So you expect to go to the University of Virginia this fall. I must say something about that place and vicinity as I am afraid you will be disappointed. I refer to the ladies of Charlottesville, for collectively or individually they merit the rank of the <u>ugliest</u> of the ugly; I could mention illustrations of the truth of this remark, but I know that you will have an opportunity of judging for yourself soon enough to your sorrow, but without a joke Charlottesville is a sweet place, and if it had such a man as Colonel Boyd to rouse public spirit, it would surpass any town in the United States so far as beauty is concerned. It may be however, the striking contrast, which exists between the ugly women and the pretty gardens and yards clothed in roses, that robes the place in apparent loveliness. After leaving Washington I was for the greater portion of my time shut up close in the cars and consequently could not see much of the country through which I passed, but I passed up the Chesapeake Bay on board a steamboat from Baltimore and they sky being clear we had a pleasant voyage; the scenery on the bay is beautiful. I stayed a very short time in New York and during my stay I must confess I appreciated the sentiment of Yankee Doodle when he "couldn't see the town for the houses".

Leaving New York about 5:30 P. M. I took passage on board a steamboat for this place where I arrived about 11 o'clock at night, so you see I lost the most interesting part of my trip on account of its being too dark to see the magnificent scenery, but what I did see before dark was truly worth seeing, and to all who enjoy mountain scenery, a trip up the Hudson would be quite a treat. The scenery along the River from this place is grand with Crow's Nest if full view and the beautiful town of Newburgh in the distance[66]. West Point is a place of great resort during the months of July and August, and at evening parade especially the space in front of camp ground is full of smiling faces and bright eyes from every part of the Union. Camp life is glorious, but it is lazy business for all except the Plebeians who have to drill in Infantry Tactics thrice a day and in Artillery once a day[67]. We have been in camp about three weeks and will return to Barracks the 28th proximo. There is a Cadet in the second class name Jerome Napoleon Bonaparte who is the best looking Cadet on the Point. He is Napoleon Bonaparte's great grandnephew[68]. There is also a grandson of Henry Clay here named Henry Clay Jr. son of Lieutenant Colonel Clay who fell in Mexico and a host of other Cadets whose only recommendations is a name rendered immortal by their ancestors, a Calhoun, a Polk, a Shunk, etc. The fourth of July here was a day of some interest. The procession was formed on parade ground in from of Camp at ten o'clock A. M. in the following order: 1. Escort of Cadets under arms, 2. Chaplain, Orator of the day, and reader of the Declaration of Independence (the two last are chosen annually by the Dialectic Society), 3. Academic Staff, 4. 1st Class, 2nd Class, 3rd Class and last 4th Class. The band played Hail Columbia, the Star-Spangled Banner, and Yankee Doodle delightfully. After the oration was delivered the procession returned to camp and 30 salutes were fired, one for each State in the Union. The oration was well written, but miserably declaimed. He had the monotonous tone of school-boy declamation which diminished in a great degree the good effect of the

---

[66] The Crow's Nest is the highest point along the Hudson River and is two miles north of West Point.
[67] Plebes are cadets in their initial year at West Point.
[68] Jerome Napoleon Bonaparte, Class of 1852, served in the French army 1854-1870

composition. Nothing at all was done in the afternoon. At night sky rockets were set off in the air until tattoo (9 o'clock).

I would be very glad to see you here at any time and if you ever take a trip to the north you must come to West Point, especially when you become a member of Congress which I hope will be soon, but you will have to change your politics if you expect to go from the district in which you now reside. I've wearied you with this nonsense long enough so I will conclude by earnestly soliciting you to excuse the scrawl as it is written soldier fashion on my knee, and to write soon and tell me all the news and how you spend your time. Give my love to Uncles James Ewell Brown and tell him I will write soon. I wrote to Brother Alex about a week ago. My love to him and Sister Mary. Your letter is the only one I have received from Virginia since I left. Continue so punctual and your letters will ever be eagerly perused by me. Remember me affectionately to Cousin Fannie and Jane. Kiss Bettie and John Brown for me, and give my best respects to M.

    Your affectionate cousin,

    James

P. S. Don't forget to direct your letter to Cadet J. E. B. Stuart, U. S. Military Academy, West Point, New York.

TO GEORGE HAIRSTON[69]

    Camp Gaines, United States Military Academy[70]

    West Point, New York, August 17, 1850

My Dear Cousin:

---

[69] George Hairston (1822-1866)

[70] Camp Gaines was named for General Edmund Gaines (1777-1849), a veteran of the Florida Indian and Mexican Wars.

I have delayed writing to you this long that I might become fully acquainted with the place and consequently better qualified to give you some idea of the Point as well as to tell you how I am pleased with my new situation. So far I know no profession more desirable than that of the soldier; indeed everything connected with the Academy has far surpassed my most sanguine expectations; the natural beauty of the situation of West Point; the picturesque mountain scenery, the magnificent view of the Hudson, the delightful River-breezes (which by the by, will not be so pleasant in the winter,); all conspire to render our life agreeable; to say nothing of other advantages afforded for intellectual culture and polish.

We have been in Camp Gaines since the 23rd of June, drilling 3 times a day in Artillery and Infantry Tactics; and we have had a glorious time; for I think I could live in Camp the remainder of my days if it remained warm enough. There have been a number of Visitors on the Point during the present Encampment, among others, Gen[era]l Scott and family, the latter generally spend the entire Summer here, Gen[era]l Paez, N. P. Willis, and a host of Honorable "M C's".[71] Miss Scott is considered one of the most expert riders in the Country, and if we judge from her frequent exercise in that art, she is fond of displaying her horsemanship (or I should have said horsewomanship). She is continually galloping her steed, which is a beautiful bay, over the plain and at evening Parade, at which there is a cannon fired, at a certain signal of the Drum. It is not uncommon to see her immediately in front of the cannon sitting erect on her "bonnie Bay", while others of the fair, of less bold nature, are stopping their ears, ready to scream and faint, but always manage to recover from their fright in time to see the Parade, while Miss

---

[71] General Winfield Scott (1786-1866) of Virginia was a general in chief of the United States Army from 1841 to 1861. Jose Antonio Paez (1790-1873) was the first president of Venezuela and in exile beginning in 1850. Nathaniel Parker Willis (1806-1867) was an author living near West Point, New York.

Scott for a while enveloped in a cloud of smoke, soon displays her white plume above it, and her steed bounds off over the Plain as if proud of his burden; you cannot wonder, Cousin George, that such chivalric spirit in Miss Scott renders her quite a Belle among the Ladies' men of the Corps among whom of course I do not number myself.

  Two years seems a long time to be separated from home and friends but if it passes off as rapidly in proportion as the last two months have to me, I will be perfectly satisfied; at that time if I am not expelled previously, and nothing else happens to the contrary. I will visit home from the 18th of June to the 28th of August and shall not fail to give you a call. The corps of Cadets had a melancholy and to me quite a novel duty to perform a few days ago. I mean the burial of an officer Capt. Spencer Norville, who having fought gallantly through the 8th and 9th of May, escaped unscathed, and returned to the bosom of his family, laden with laurels and the heartfelt gratitude of his Countrymen, but nursing at the same time the seeds of that disease which finally proved fatal to his career on earth; he was buried with all the pomp and solemnity, attendant upon the burial of a distinguished officer, and gallant hero.[72]

  Camp Gaines claims for its site the loveliest and most romantic spot on the plain; it being in immediate vicinity of the ruins of Fort Clinton, on the verge of the Hudson, a little above Koscuisko's Garden which is a beautiful spot, in the wildest nook of jutting cliffs, and covered with prickly-pears and cedar, with a delightful spring in the center enclosed in a bowl of white marble bearing the inscription simply "Kosciusko".[73] Near the garden is the Koscuisko monument and the one erected to "Dade and his command" who fell in the Florida campaign.[74]

---

[72] JEBS is referring to the battles at Resaca de la Palma and Palo Alto from the Mexican War in 1846.
[73] Between the Hudson River and Fort Clinton at West Point was a rock garden designed by Tadeusz Kosciusko, a Polish engineer in the American Revolution.

Fort Putnam, appropriately termed the "Gibraltar of America" lifts its grey ruins above a neighboring height, in full view of the encampment.[75] We expect to return to Barracks on the 28th inst[ant] to commerce study.

Mr. Chevalier called here to see me sometime in July and stayed a day; he seemed very much pleased with the place.[76] It would gratify me exceedingly to see any of my friends here during my stay, and hope if you ever undertake a trip to the North, that you will not fail to make this one of your stopping places, the months of July, Aug[ust] and Sep[tember] are generally the most interesting periods to visit the Point.

I hope to hear from you soon. Give me love to Aunt Ruth, Cousin Sam Harden and all of Uncle Sam's family.[77]

Forgive this scrawl, as you must know that there are no conveniences for writing in Camp, for every man's knee is his desk. Remember me to Lieut[enant] Cabell when you see him and believe me as every yours.[78]

Affectionately,

J. E. B. Stuart

P. S. Address your letter to "Cadet J. E. B. Stuart, U. S. M. Academy, West Point, N. Y. " As there are two P. offices here.

JEBS

---

[74] Francis L. Dade lost his command of 110 in the Seminole War in 1835.
[75] Fort Putnam was near West Point during the American Revolution
[76] Reverend Nicholas Chevalier was married to JEBS sister Bethenia Pannill (1819-1905).
[77] Ruth Stovall Hairston Wilson Hairston was the daughter of Peter Hairston and Alcey Perkins. Samuel Harden Hairston married Alcey Hairston, sister of letter recipient George Hairston.
[78] William Lewis Cabell (1827-1911) was an 1850 graduate of the USMA and friend of the Hairston family. He served as a Brigadier General for the CSA.

Elizabeth Letcher Pannill Stuart, mother of J. E. B. Stuart

TO ALEXANDER STUART BROWN

United States Military Academy

West Point, New York, October 21, 1850

Dear Cousin,

I embrace an early opportunity to answer your affectionate letter, which I received a few days ago in order to apologize for the folly of my former letter. I was wrong for even insinuating such a thing as you not being desirous of hearing from me when you have always evinced so much interest in my progress, but my folly was, in expressing to you, what I really never entertained in my own mind, dissatisfaction with the sentiments embodied in your kind letter. Now this was done, I assure you, more from the want of something to write than with any view to censure and I had no sooner mailed the letter than a moment's reflection convinced me of its impropriety and was sorry that I had written it. But I am truly gratified to see from your letter that you were disposed to look over my fault, well-deserving another mode of treatment far different from the one it received, which dispositions on your part affords me another of the many proofs of your fidelity as a friend. So, let the affair be buried in forgetfulness.

I was glad to hear you were so well pleased with the University and we so admirably situated for study and improvement. The University is indeed a lovely spot and so is its vicinity.[79] I know I shall never regret my taking that in on my way to this place. I became acquainted with several students whose names I have forgotten with the exception of young Fulton, an intimate friend of Richard Sanders.[80] I was also introduced to the Misses Omohundro of the Monticello House.[81] If you

---

[79] The University of Virginia at Charlottesville, Virginia.
[80] Richard Sanders of Max Meadows, Wythe County, Virginia, graduated from UVA in 1849 and became a physician.
[81] John R. "Texas Jack" Omohundro (1846-1880) grew up south of

are acquainted with them, please deliver my respects when you see them again. I received letters from Pa and John since they have been in Richmond; both were well. Nothing of much importance has transpired since I last wrote. We had the pleasure of a visit from Colonel Bliss a week or two ago, and we are now looking for _____ Bey of the Sublime Porte accompanied by the Honorable Daniel Webster. The former is on a tour through our country and visiting the principal military posts of the government. He is the first Turkish Minister ever sent to this country. We have orders to receive him with a salute of thirteen guns and review of the troops. I am now rooming with Bingham, (of) Indiana and Rogers of Smyth County Virginia, both very studious and clever fellows, so I am well situated for studying.[82] Time with me flies rapidly so my furlough will soon roll round. I will be somewhere in Virginia, if alive, on the 25th of June 1852.

I hope Cousin Sandy will be of service to me in the event of my being found deficient in conduct or studies and sent away. Our first examination will take place the first week of January next when about 25 or our number will be sent home.

I will much obliged to you for the numbers of the Jefferson Monument Magazine. I sent you a copy of the New York Herald last week. Write soon and pardon the scrawl. I will take pleasure in answering your letters punctually.

The bugle has blown and I must conclude. Your truly affectionate Cousin and sincere friend,

---

Charlottesville near Palmyra. He scouted for Stuart in the Civil War in 1864. One of his sisters, Elizabeth was eight when Stuart visited Charlottesville and another Arabella was one and might be the Misses that Stuart refers too.
[82] Judson D. Bingham (1831-1909) of New York graduated ninth in the class of 1854, served in the U. S. Army until retiring in 1895 at rank of Brigadier General. Charles G. Rogers (1830-1888) of North Carolina graduated eleventh, resigned in 1855, and taught math in Tennessee before and after the Civil War.

Alexander Hugh Holmes Stuart was a cousin of J. E. B. Stuart.
TO ALEXANDER STUART BROWN
   United States Military Academy, West Point, New York

October 25, 1850

Dear Cousin,

I received yours of the 21st instant about an hour ago and now hasten to comply with your request by sending you the manuscript copy of your able address on "Ambition". Alick, I don't mean to flatter you, but candidly there are parts of that speech which in my humble judgment, will compare with the best oratorical productions of the country. I might _____ you reference to the glory of Napoleon and the concluding appeal to the Society. No other considerations could induce me to part with it, other than enabling you to establish a reputation at the University, which will last you and be of use to you as long as you remain an inhabitant of Virginia, and my confidence in your promise to return it in the course of a few months. I congratulate you heartily on your success in your first attempt. Your chameleon metaphor is beautiful.

I hope you will not consider it presumption in me, but attribute it rather to my anxiety for your success to suggest an amendment to one part of your address. I mean the part concluding about Napoleon's grandeur of genius. Instead of what you have I would suggest the following.

"and all, save the throne of God and company

of Heaven, shall have passed away",

"And like the baseless fabric of a vision,

Left not a rock behind. "[83]

Now my reasons for it are these; first, nothingness is a _____ an awkward word to be at the end of a sentence, and second, I think a quotation from Shakespeare where it is appropriate, is very admissible in a speech. Now I think you will concur with me in this amendment.

---

[83] Shakespeare, The Tempest, Act 4, Scene 1

Not Signed

TO ALEXANDER STUART BROWN

United States Military Academy, West Point, New York,
January 24, 1851

Dear Cousin,

I have been surprised at your delay but hope that you will atone for it soon. I have time to write only a line or two to inform you that for reasons pretty much the same as those offered by yourself, you would much oblige me by enclosing to me my speech on "The Triumphs of True Principles[84]" as soon as you can conveniently. I am required to write several compositions in the course of a few weeks and I find it very irksome business even when I have the time to spare, but at this time I am kept too busy to devote the time requisite to writing. I hope you will comply with my request. You can have it again as soon as we meet if you desire it. I came out pretty well at the Examination. There are 73 in our class and I stand 8th. I commenced French last week and I will write you a French letter in the course of 1851.

I remain always your affectionate cousin
and devoted friend, James

P.S. My last letter to you was dated October 22nd, 1850 except the one enclosing your speech, which I do not count.

---

[84] This speech was used by both cousins and Stuart used it at Emory and Henry and at West Point. Brown used it at the University of Virginia.

J. E. B. Stuart circa 1854.

TO GEORGE HAIRSTON,
Berry Hill, Virginia

    United States Military Academy

    West Point, New York, March 6, 1851

Dear Cousin,

    I received your very interesting and truly welcome letter last September. I have delayed answering it so long that I am almost ashamed to do it now; but I hope you will not cast me aside as an unprincipled reprobate, at least till you have given me an unbiased hearing.

    Your favor reached me soon after we had left our pleasant quarters in Camp Gaines for barracks, and were preparing to enter upon the dull career of the student. True, I could have answered you immediately, but times were so dull, that it would have been impossible for me to communicate anything of the least interest to you; so I concluded to wait until I could find something worth writing; and thus I have been procrastinating from day to day till (how strange to say!) six months have glided past, and Cousin George's letter is still unanswered. But I assure you my intentions were good, and if I had been told last September that your letter would not be answered till now, I would not have believed it. Now taking into consideration the rectitude of my intentions I trust you will overlook the past and write soon so as to afford me an opportunity to retrieve my honor.

    We came into barracks on the first of September, and since that time "hard study" has been our constant watchword. I used to think that I had some idea of what hard study was, at least my idea of it was that it was something to be avoided as much as possible which before I came here I succeeded at admirably, but on coming here I found that it was necessary to cultivate a more intimate acquaintance with it or else come out wanting at the Examination. So I turned into studying pretty hard.

Our semi=annual Examination came off last January at which our class was arranged according to individual merit in the different branches of study, that is; the Cadet who was most proficient in Mathematics, for instance, was placed first in that department, the next best, second, and so on to the worst. There were in our class before Jan[uary] 94, of whom 22 were found deficient and sent home; reducing it to 72; among the last number I had the good fortune to be placed. I stood in Mathematics sixth, in English Studies, embracing Blair's Rhetoric and English Grammar, fifteenth and in average or general merit, eighth. I came out upon the whole pretty well, much better than I anticipated, but I take no credit whatever to myself for my success, for you know, a man deserves no praise for doing what he is obliged to do. Immediately after our Examination we set in again to study, without a moment's respite and we will be busily employed at it till June when we will again pitch our Camp. In January we commenced French, which I am very pleased with and will endeavor to acquire a thorough knowledge of it.

The more I see of West Point, the better I am pleased with the Institution, indeed no consideration would make me willing exchange my present situation for another. Placed as I am, at an Institution which is the foster-child of the Nation, enjoying privileges eminently superior to any other in the world, and presenting inducements the most favorable for intellectual improvement and success in the world, add to these, the surpassing loveliness of the spot by nature, its picturesque mountain scenery, its thrilling associations with the struggle of our forefathers, and I would be worse than brute, were I else than pleased.

My health has been remarkably fine since I have been here; I think the climate suits me better than that of Virginia. One would think that a place situated as this is, in the heart of free-soil-Yankeedom was strongly tainted with that spirit, but quite the contrary is the fact, for there is a strong Southern feeling prevalent on the Point no doubt far more than Mr. Van Buren ever cherished.[85] A majority of the officers and Professors are from the South, and nearly all the ladies. Many are from Virginia. But we are far from entertaining towards each other as marked antipathy as the times would suggest were we "cits", but there seems to be a sentiment of mutual forbearance, in a word, with us all is harmony. True, particular sects are more intimate than others for you know that "birds of a feather will roost together"; but as a general thing we, in the language of one worthy of being quoted, "know no East, no West, no North, no South".

I would like very much for Henry to become my successor; tell him I hope he will come to see me while here at any rate, and have a chance to see more of the place; I am confident that a sight of the place would make him more anxious than ever to become a Cadet.[86] L[ieutenan]t Cabell took this in his route to Jefferson Barracks M[iss]o[uri]. That Post is considered the most preferable of any. I have not heard from him since he left. From the short acquaintance I had, I think him a very clever fellow. I subscribe cheerfully to your remarks in regard to Miss Scot, though I must say I admire her horsemanship rather more than her Ladyship. I received a letter from Lummie the other day.[87] She said that Aunt Agnes and Cousins Sam H and A were on a visit to Mississippi.[88] I suppose by this time you are beginning to expect their return. I am glad to see that Dr. Averett is a candidate for re-election and

---

[85] Martin Van Buren (1782-1862) of nearby Kinderhook, New York, was the eighth President of the United States of America and had run in 1846 on the antislavery Free-Soil party.
[86] Henry Hairston (1836-1862) was the brother of the letter recipient George Hairston.
[87] Columbia Lafayette Stuart (1831-1857) was the sister of JEBS.
[88] Agnes John Peter Wilson Hairston was the mother of the letter recipient George Hairston. Samuel Harden Hairston and Alcey were siblings of George Hairston.

I sincerely wish him success.[89] I fear he made a sacrifice in appointing me which will endanger his success, for you know that the Taliaferro's are a numerous family Franklin.

I do not know that the Judge would be influenced by such considerations, but if he were, he might defeat the Doctor. My acquaintance with him was very short but I was much pleased with his manner. I would have delivered your message to Mrs. Floyd had I had an opportunity, but she was in Tazewell during my stay in Wythe.[90] Give my love to Aunt Ruth and Cousin Ruth, tell the latter that, with her permission, I will come to see Miss Agnes during my furlough in 52.

Please write as soon as convenient and excuse this scrawl, and I promise to do better next time.

> I remain, Dear Cousin,
> Your sincere friend and cousin
> J. E. B. Stuart

---

[89] Dr. Thomas Hamlet Averett of Halifax County, Virginia, a Democrat, served in the 31st and 32nd Congresses of the United States of America and appointed JEBS to the USMA.

[90] Tazewell and Wythe counties are located in southwest Virginia.

Painting of Archibald Stuart with damage reportedly done by one of George Stoneman's troopers during a raid on Saltville, Virginia, in December 1864.

TO ARCHIBALD STUART
United States Military Academy
West Point, New York, March 25, 1851

Dear Pa,

I received your affectionate letter the other day and in obedience to your request take an early opportunity to answer it, though I can muster nothing of the least interest to write. Mr. Chambliss[91] and myself are quite well. He has just this moment returned from cavalry exercise rigged out in dragoon style. Spring is fast approaching and our drills and parades begin to animate the plain. A week ago the melancholy duty devolved upon us of consigning to the tomb the remains of another officer, the late Captain Henry[92], who having fought through the Florida and Mexican Campaigns, breathed his last in New York, and was conveyed to this place to be buried with military honors in the Cadet Cemetery. He was said to be a great favorite in the army and was the author of "Campaign Sketches". The ceremony of a military burial is very solemn as well as imposing.

We would be very happy to see you and Mr. Chambliss here some time during your term at Richmond and if possible at our June examination. Don't you think you can come? I think you would enjoy the trip. I received a letter from John Stuart at the same time I received yours. I was truly glad to hear that he had obtained so good a situation with Dr. Headen. I also received a letter this morning from Sister Bethenia; all were well. I am getting to like the place better every day. Our class commenced Descriptive Geometry the other day which, being altogether new to me, I found rather difficult at first, but now I like it

---

[91] John R. Chambliss, Sr. (1809-1875) father of Confederate Brigadier General John R. Chambliss, Jr. (1833-1864)
[92] William Seton Henry (1816-1851)

better than Elementary Geometry. We are progressing rapidly with it. I have not heard from home or Wythe County in a long time. Soon after I wrote to you I received my warrant from the War Department which I enclosed in a letter to Ma, and I took the oath of allegiance to "Uncle Sam". So I wish you to understand that I no longer belong to you. Write when convenient and excuse the scrawl. The drum will soon beat for parade and I must hasten to conclude.

      Still your devoted son, James

TO ARCHIBALD STUART

  United States Military Academy, West Point, New York,
  June 2, 1851

Dear Pa:

  I have stolen a leisure hour this morning for the purpose of answering your affectionate letter which I received last week. Our examination commences today and preparations are now busily making to receive the Board of Visitors in military style. Today will be taken up with the reception and other preliminary matters and the examination of the first class in Engineering will begin tomorrow. I would be perfectly delighted to see you here during the progress of the examination, and when I reflect how easy a matter it will be to pair off with any member for a few days I can't see what can deter you from coming. You wish to know "what time will be most advantageous for your visit". I am of the opinion that during the next week will be the most interesting period but any time will do during the examination. I hope you will not let so good an opportunity pass. I would like very much for you to see something of military life. My time will soon be up and I am obliged to hasten to a conclusion. Mr. Chambliss is quite well, and in ecstasies about going on furlough. I wish him a pleasing one. My respects to Edwin Parker. I received a letter from Sister Mary Headen a few days since; all were well. I suppose you hear from those parts oftener than I. I have not heard from Brother Alex since Christmas. Excuse the scrawl. I am quite well.

I remain in haste your affectionate son,

James

TO ARCHIBALD STUART

      Camp Brady, West Point, New York.,

      July 22, 1851

My Dear Pa,

      Your kind letter arrived yesterday. I thank you very much for the remittance you were pleased to make me, and will devote it today to the purchase of a supply of gloves and collars. You need not send me any more as the sum you sent will last me till next June. I will endeavor to appreciate your kind admonition in regard to debt to my utmost. It is bad enough for a young man of fortune when setting out in life to become involved and encumbered by a load of debt, but how much worse is if for one without fortune when about to launch into life to find at the first step, debt. I am determined to free myself from mine as soon as possible. I am not at all afraid but what I can discharge it as soon as I enter the Army but Brother Alex needs it now, and if by foregoing the pleasure of returning on furlough I can in any manner help to discharge it, I will do it cheerfully. It is not because I care little about home and friends, for I think I love them better than anyone else.

      You spoke in one of your former letters of having had a daguerreotype taken for me. I am a thousand times obliged to you for it, and hope I shall shortly have the infinite gratification of holding in my hands so kind a token from you. I prize such a gift very highly. I knew with what solicitude I watch for it at the Post Office, you would have sent it before this. The War Department will send you shortly a catalogue, or, as it is her called, Register of the Academy from which you will learn many little interesting particulars about the place. You have no idea what a pleasure your correspondence affords me. I look forward to the adjournment sine die of the convention with far different views from most Virginians. They are glad of it. I am very sorry for then I shall be deprived of your interesting and affectionate letters, for you will be so busy when you return home that you will have little or no time to think of me much less write. As I have heard nothing for some time in regard to Uncle Brown's[93] health, I take it for granted that he has recovered. Please give my best respects to your Parker when you see him, and tell him that I will be pleased to hear from him. I hope you will write to me again before you leave Richmond. We had the honor of a visit from General Scott and Governor Hunt[94] a few days ago. We greeted them with a salute of 15 guns each. Please write soon and excuse this imperfect scrawl.

      I still remain your devoted son,
      James

TO GEORGE HAIRSTON

  Camp Brady, West Point, New York[95]
  August 13, 1851

Dear Cousin,

  My delay in answering your kind letter you must not attribute to willful neglect, for I assure you nothing has been farther from my intention; but time has passed away so fast this Encampment that I was unconscious of the delay. I have spent Camp Brady very agreeable

---

[93] Judge James E. Brown, father of Alexander Stuart Brown.
[94] Governor Washington Hunt (1811-1867) of New York (1851-52),
[95] Camp Brady honored General Hugh Brady, veteran of the War of 1812 and Mexican War.

indeed so far, much more so than the last Encampment, for I assure you there is a great difference between a third Classman and a "Plebe". I have been fortunate enough to receive the appointment of Corporal in the Corps of Cadets the third in rank, and as such, have been acting as Orderly Sergeant of Company "A" during this Encampment, as the proper Orderly Sergeant is now on furlough. Occupying a Post of so great responsibility I have been granted many privileges, which are denied the rest of the Corps, so upon the whole I have had a splendid time. I would be delighted to see you here on the 28th, as that is the day on which the ceremony of striking camp takes place, which is truly a magnificent scene.

I determined as the beginning of the Encampment not to become acquainted with any ladies during its continuance. But my resolve however firm when withstanding the smiles of yankeedom, melted away when the warm sunshine of a lovely Virginia Girl's eye shone upon it. I have an intimate friend in the corps named Jno [John] Pegram of Richmond who is decidedly the best hearted fellow I ever knew.[96] A few days ago his mother and sister came to see him and I was introduced to them. I found Mrs. P. an excellent lady of the Old Virginia stamp.[97] As far as Miss Mary Pegram without saying anything disrespectful of her, I beg leave to state that I will not insure the self-possession of my heart, for it is my humble opinion that it has left its old habitation.[98] That Miss Mary is intelligent, fascinating, beautiful and modest and that she is a Virginian is an enumeration of by no means half of her excellent qualities. She told me she was intimately acquainted with Miss Sallie

---

[96] John Pegram (1832-1865) graduated the USMA with JEBS in the class of 1854 and served in the U. S. Army and Confederate Army dying in battle on February 6, 1865.
[97] Mrs. James West Pegram, mother of John, Willie and Mary Pegram.
[98] Miss Mary Pegram, sister of John and Willie Pegram(1841-1865).

James Ewell Brown, father of Alexander Stuart Brown, the brother-in-law of Archibald Stuart and the man for whom Confederate General James Ewell Brown Stuart was named.

Broadnax before her death and spoke in high terms of her character. She says also that she was a schoolmate of Miss Mary Broadnax and Cousin Ruth and Alcey at Mr. McKenzie's school in Richmond (It was either McKenzie's or some name very much like it).[99] She left here on yesterday and I have been nearly dead with the "blues" ever since. She gave me a flower which is now in a glass on my table before me (the Orderly Sergeants are allowed tables) and I have thought several times of throwing it (the flower) away for I can't look towards it without a return of the "blues". To speak candidly, I never knew any one whom I esteemed more on so short an acquaintance than Mrs. Pegram and her daughter, I hated to part with them as much as if they had been intimate friends from childhood. They gave me a very pressing invitation to call on them on my way home next June, which I shall certainly do if I have the pleasure of going. Miss Mary will return to witness the "finale" on the 28th. With the exception of my present attack of the blues, my spirits have been unruffled since the Encampment began.

Professor Phillips of whom you spoke did come on but I did not have any opportunity of forming an opinion of his excellences as he merely looked on, as did the others of the Board with out saying a word.[100] I came out in June exactly where I stood in January. The Examination in June is quite an interesting time at the Point, and all who paid us a visit last June seemed highly pleased. We look forward to next June with the fondest anticipations, indeed there is no period in a man's life cherished dearer and wished nearer than a cadet's furlough. I have not yet determined whether to go on furlough or not. It would afford me

---

[99] The Broadnax family, usually spelled Brodnax, were related to the Hairston family. Jane Mackenzie's school for girls was at Fifth and Franklin streets in Richmond, Virginia.
[100] Professor James Phillips of the University of North Carolina at Chapel Hill.

indescribable pleasure, but under certain circumstances I will decline accepting it.

I have not heard from any of my friends for some time. I will write to Lummie very soon. Please give my love to all of my friends, to Cousins Aunts and Uncles. I hope you will forgive this scrawl, as I have the blues so dreadfully that I can't frame the first idea, please write soon and I will try and write you a longer and more interesting letter.

Gen[eral] Scott has paid us a visit this summer, though his daughter has not.

I am still your Devoted cousin

J. E. B. Stuart

TO ALEXANDER STUART BROWN

United States Military Academy, West Point, New York

December 13, 1851

Dear Cousin

The long silence on your part which has followed my letter of last May is inexplicable. Since then you have been home, seen all our old friends, and had many other things to write about which would interest me so much, yet you have not deigned to say a word. I got along first rate through the encampment during which I had the honor of Acting Orderly Sergeant. I was made a Corporal, the 3rd in rank, in June and am still one. So far I have been getting along pretty well in military matters but I fear my heart it irrevocably gone. We have nothing of interest here. I suppose you have heard of Kossuth's[101] debut in New York and no doubt you have long since formed your opinion of the man. My own is that he is a mere demagogical humbug and the United States will regret the

---

[101] Lajos Kossuth (1802-1894), Hungarian revolutionary toured America in 1851-52.

reception given him yet, more than they regretted that given to Dickens.[102] (Mark my Prophecy)!!

I expect to go on furlough in June next. If you expect to be at the university at that time I will take it in my route and call on you. Lieutenant Jones an officer stationed here, originally from Charlottesville, is now on leave of absence. Have you seen him? I have not heard from any of my Wythe [County] friends in a great while. How are you doing at the university? What do you think of [Virginia Governor] Johnson's[103] triumph? Please write soon and excuse this hasty scrawl. I will write you a long letter next time.

Signature cut off

TO GEORGE HAIRSTON

United States Military Academy, West Point, New York
December 25, 1851

Dear Cousin:

I know of no method of spending this joyous festivity, which will afford me more pleasure than answering your kind letter of the third instant. With you Christmas is anything but a dull day, but with us it is quite so, it seems really to be a blank day so far as external demonstrations are a test, for before twelve o'clock nearly every Cadet will be locked in the embrace of Morpheus[104], and thus dream away the glorious day. I have always enjoyed the reputation of being pretty lazy, but it must be said to my credit that of all things I abhor being compelled to do nothing most. So I will for the present bid my "companions in arms" pleasant slumbers and imagine myself seated with you "tete a tete"

---

[102] Charles Dickens (1812-1870) toured America in 1842 and wrote *American Notes For General Circulation*, in which he condemned slavery.
[103] Joseph Johnson (1795-1877) was the 32nd Governor of Virginia (1852-1856).
[104] Morpheus was the Greek god of dreams.

around a large Christmas fire. Well Cousin George I wish you a merry Christmas. I believe to-day is a time appointed by Aunt Ruth for all her Grandchildren to visit her, if so I know you will have a fine time.

I suppose you have heard of the late commotion created by the arrival of Gov[ernor] Kossuth in N[ew] York.[105] This and the "coup d'etat" of Louis Napoleon[106] are the current topics of conversation in the Corps; and from what I can gather, they are by no means inclined to join a crusade to republicanize Europe, but still, we stand ready to obey orders.

The Cadet whom you saw at the Springs is named Terrill; he enjoys the reputation of being the ugliest man in the Corps; and so I hope you will not consider him as a fair specimen, so far as looks are concerned.[107] But he is a very good-hearted fellow if he is ugly. I am very much gratified to hear Dr. Averetts election, especially as he was elected by such an increased majority. My wish is that he may long prove the same able Representative, which his past actions show him to be.

I would be very glad indeed for Cousin Henry to succeed me as Cadet and think a military life would suit him. I believe four years training at West Point would be the making of him. It would be the means of strengthening his constitution, establishing his health, making him, both physically and mentally, emphatically a man. For one to succeed here, all that is required is an ordinary mind and application, the latter is by far the most important and desirable of the two. For men of rather obtuse intellect, by indomitable perseverance have been known to graduate with honor; while some of the greatest geniuses of the Country

---

[105] Lajos Kossuth (1802-1894) had fled Hungry in 1851.
[106] Charles Louis Napoleon Bonaparte was President of France (1848-1852). He later ruled as Napoleon III (1852-1870).
[107] William R. Terrill (1834 -1862) of Virginia graduated USMA in 1853 and was killed at Perryville, Kentucky, during the Civil War in 1862.

have been found deficient, for want of application; Edgar A. Poe for instance.

Our semi-annual Examination commences on the 1st prox [imo], which it is thought will terminate the military career of about 20 or 30 "Plebes". After this we have some more study and then furlough. I heard from Lieut[enant] Cabell not long since; he was at Fort Arbuckle, Texas frontier.[108] I wrote him to try and get a leave also next Summer, but he is in such active service keeping the Indians in check I doubt whether he applies.

You have been more fortunate than I, to hear from Cousin P. and Lummie for they have deigned to write since they left Floyd.[109] I reckon however they are so much absorbed with that smart boy of theirs that they think about little else; on such a plea I excuse them.[110] I am glad to see Democracy so triumphant in Virginia, and hope it may continue so.[111] I received a letter from Bro[ther] A.[112] yesterday which informs me that Miss Eliza Stuart has arrived in Wytheville, and that Pa is elected to the senate.[113] I see to from Richmond paper that Dr. Headen and Uncle George Hairston are also elected to the Legislature; so it seems that we will be well represented in that body.[114]

---

[108] Fort Arbuckle created in 1850 was in southern Oklahoma until closed in 1870.
[109] Floyd, Virginia, was home to Dr. Headen and John D. Stuart.
[110] Peter W. Hairston had married JEBS sister Columbia and their son Samuel (1850-1869) had recently been born.
[111] Virginia had chosen governor, lieutenant governor, judges, and other state and local officials had been elected by popular vote for the first time in 1851
[112] William Alexander Stuart.
[113] Eliza Stuart was an infant daughter of WAS that died in infancy. Archibald Stuart was elected to the Virginia Senate in 1852.
[114] Dr. Tazewell Headen represented Floyd County in the Virginia House of Delegates and was married to JEBS sister Mary. George Hairston (1784-1863) was an uncle of the letter recipient.

Our bands have commenced their winter Concerts which attract many of the Fair to our Halls every Saturday evening. The music and the smiles of the Ladies together have a tendency to dispel for a time the gloom of winter, but it soon returns with redoubled power. The weather is extremely cold today and has been so for some weeks. Our class have been drilled in riding all this year and ought by June to be quite expert horsemen. It is great fun for us from the South, but you ought to see what ridiculous figures these Yankees cut on horseback. Some of them never mounted a horse before. We have excellent horses. But you will have an opportunity of judging of my horsemanship next summer. I expect to start on furlough about the 18th of June. I will stay a day or two at Washington with Cousin Sandy, in Richmond with Jno. [John] Pegram, in Lynchburg with Uncle Chiswell, at the University with Cousin A. Brown and in Christiansburg and Wytheville with my relatives at these points.[115] I will not be able to reach home then till about the 1st of July. I would not be deprived of the pleasure of seeing you all, on furlough for anything.

Give my love to Aunt Ruth, Aunt Agnes and the balance. Please present my compliments to Miss Agnes. I believe Cousin Sam Harden and A. are now in Mississippi, but I hope they will have returned before next summer. My love to Cousin Henry and tell him he must be a Cadet by all means. Tell him I Have a great deal to tell him about West Point but will reserve it until I see him. Is he as fond of hunting as ever? I am afraid I have wearied you already by so much nonsense so I will relieve you, by bidding you "good day" and transporting myself with reluctance from your presence and Christmas fire to the stern and cold reality of Barrack life; but be sure I leave with you the lasting regards of

---

[115] Cousin Sandy is Alexnader H. H. Stuart, Alexander Stuart Brown, Chiswell Dabney.

Your devoted Cousin
J. E. B. Stuart

P. S. The Thermometer was 11 degrees below Zero to day at 11 A. M. in a room without fire. Please answer this scrawl soon and I will do better next time.

J. E. B. S

TO GEORGE HAIRSTON

United States Military Academy, West Point, New York
April 13, 1852

Cousin George

No doubt you already think that I have forgotten you, and that my delay in answering your letter has proceeded from deliberate neglect, but such, be assured, is far from being the case. I have treated you precisely as I have treated all my correspondents for the last month or two, though I admit you least deserved such treatment, and I promise henceforth that you shall have no reason to complain.

We have just past one of the severest winters ever felt even in this cold region; the snow, which fell to the depth of six or eight inches the other day, is still on the ground in places unexposed to the sun. But in spite of such a state of affairs the Point seems determined not to be behind hand, and wears a fresher green every day; indeed spring with all its joys, spring, which makes West Point the loveliest of spots, is fast approaching. But what makes her arrival at present a peculiar source of pleasure and gratulation to us third Classmen is the fact of her being the joyful harbinger of Furlough. She gives new energy to our hopes of realizing that optimum of our life. I will not trouble you however with an account of all the studied plans which we have formed, and the magnificent castles which we have erected in the air by feasting our imaginations on the joys of delusive anticipation that never fails

> To tinge with rainbow hues our future skies,
> And bid each thought suggest a paradise;
> To give to every hope a fairer tint,
> And melt with rapture e'en a heart of flint, (Pardon the rhyme)

For such a subject would doubtless be uninteresting to any one else, while a Cadet might hang enchanted over the thought forever. He reveres it as a sacred bequeathment, clings to it with a consciousness that it is something, which comes but once, and once gone, is gone forever. For several weeks past I have thought more of my friends away than usual. I will consider myself quite happy should I be spared to see them all once more. And it will be a source of the greatest pleasure to pay you a visit during my holiday. I often think of the pleasant hours I have spent with Aunt Ruth and yourself, and have only to regret that they have been so few.

I received a long letter from Lieut[enant] Cabell a short time since. He was then at Fort Arbuckle, Chickasaw Nation, and gave me quite an interesting account of his post and the surrounding country. He is perfectly delighted with the army, and advises me by all means to become an officer. He belongs to "7th Infantry" one of the most preferable situations in the army; in the midst of woods and Indians fifty miles from a white dwelling. The principal amusement is hunting every description of game from the partridge to the wolf. He did not say when he would again visit Virginia but said that he would be sure to select the winter season.

I suppose your mind is by this time completely absorbed by the Presidential question. So far as I am able to judge I have my preferences in favor of "Young Democracy" but I am afraid that the old Fogys will being him out second best at Baltimore.[116] President making and politics in general are things, which Cadets allow to trouble them very little. We have a few of the chivalry as well as some rank abolitionists but they take very good care to keep quiet.

I have been looking around for a Plan for Cousin Peter but find nothing new or odd except some Gothic coops; I would send him a plan of them but am afraid that he would be insulted.[117] I see that Hon[orable] William L. Goggin has been appointed one of the Board of Visitors from Virginia in the Graduating class; there is one however who was born in Virginia.[118] There are several Virginians in our Class and all doing well, for out of the 13 Cadets in the 1st section of Mathematics, 5 are Virginians.[119] Tell Cousin Henry he must not give up the idea of "the buttons". Give my love to aunt Ruth Aunt, Agnes and Cousin Ruth and the rest. Please present my compliments to Miss Agnes. Answer me soon and I will reply punctually. Excuse want of interest.

                              Yours truly and affectionately
                              J. E. B. Stuart

---

[116] The Democratic National Convention was choosing between James Buchanan, Lewis Cass and Stephen A. Douglas in 1852, but Franklin Pierce won the nomination and became President of the United States.

[117] JEBS had been viewing architectural books for Peter Wilson Hairston plantation Cooleemee.

[118] William Leftwich Goggin of Bedford County, Virginia, served several terms in the United States House of Representatives.

[119] The five Virginians are George W. C. Lee, John Pegram, Milton T. Carr, George A. Gordon, and J.E.B.Stuart.

Archibald Stuart, father of J. E. B. Stuart (Cecil Richardson)

TO ALEXANDER STUART BROWN

United States Military Academy, West Point, New York

April 20, 1852

My Dear Cousin,

I have been intending to answer your very affectionate letter for some time, but somehow I was always deterred from it.

This evening, however, I am determined to redeem my promise by informing you that I am well if nothing else. Spring has at length returned and our drills and parades already begin to enliven the Plain.

I am getting along about as usual though I can't hope to stand as high in June next as last.

Furlough is but a month or two off now, and of course we can think of nothing else. We will get about the 17th of June. At what time is your Commencement? I would like to reach you in time to witness it. I suppose you hear from home as often I do. From what I hear I believe there is little doubt entertained of Uncle Brown's and Brother Alec's re-election. It will all be over before we arrive home and I don't regret it. I believe D. H. Hoge, Esquire is the only opponent (formally announced) to Uncle Brown's. Uncle Brown, I believe, is well known in every county of his circuit except Floyd County which I expect will give him a large majority, for Doctor Headen has a great deal of influence among the people, who not being acquainted with the candidates will be in a great measure influenced by his vote.

Honorable William L. Goggin has been appointed by the President a Visitor to attend our ensuing examination. The Visitorship is of little importance as all it requires of a man is to look on, but if affords him an excellent opportunity of becoming thoroughly acquainted with the internal economy and fixtures of the Academy which he would not otherwise obtain. I was mightily in hopes that the President [Fillmore] would appoint someone with whom I am acquainted for besides the pleasure it would afford me to meet an acquaintance, it would be the mans of releasing me from a good deal of duty if I had an acquaintance on the Board. I trust we shall have a fine time together next summer. Remember me to any of my friends who may be at the university, and write soon to your devoted cousin.

Jim

P. S. Will you have completed your course of study this term? – J.

TO ARCHIBALD STUART

United States Military Academy, West Point, New York
May 21, 1852

Dear Pa,

I received your kind letter enclosing the check for $40.00 and bill for $10.00. I am very much obliged to you for your trouble.

I was in hopes that the Legislature would sit until about the 23rd proximo so that we could go home together. I have not heard yet whether or not the motion for adjournment on 31st passed the Senate. If it should I can't help from reminding you what an excellent opportunity you will have for visiting the Point. I assure you it is well worth the trouble to be her during the examination, and I hope you will give the matter a favorable consideration.

I am quite well and doing about as well as usual. I begin to look upon furlough now as something tangible since it will only be two or three weeks before I make a launch for home, especially as I have no money in my pocket for the occasion. I have received two letters of late, the one from Cousin Peter and the other from Mr. Chevalier; the former announcing the arrival into this world of Mr. Archibald Stuart Hairston[120]

---

[120] Archibald Stuart Hairston (1852-1853) was the second child of Peter and

and the latter that of another young gentleman whose name was not yet given. If Judge Baldwin should die before I leave, don't you think it would be best for me to put off my call on Cousin Sandy [Alexander H. H. Stuart][121] until my return in August? Much the cheapest and best route for me is via the Roanoke to Richmond, and if I conclude not to stop in Washington in going, I will go that route. I hope you will write to me again before June and let me know your views on the subject above mentioned. Excuse this miserable apology for a letter for I have very bad pen and worse paper. I presume you have not heard anything of Miss Pegram. I fear she will be in New Jersey while I am in Richmond and consequently I will not have the pleasure of seeing her.

I am still your affectionate son,
James

TO ELIZABETH LETCHER PANNILL STUART

United States Military Academy, West Point, New York
September 1, 1852

Dear Ma,

In compliance with the promise which you were pleased to exact, I began this letter as soon as matters have assumed a more settled form. I arrived here safely at 11:30 AM on 28th ultimo. I remained at Wytheville a day or two longer than I expected when I left home, owing to my having ascertained from Colonel Boyd that a new arrangement had been made by which I could reach New York in three days instead of six as I expected. I was sorry that I was ignorant of this arrangement when I

Columbia L. Stuart Hairston.

[121] Alexander Hugh Holmes Stuart (1807-1891) of Staunton, Augusta County, Virginia, was a cousin of J. E. B. Stuart, also descended from Judge Archibald Stuart. AHHHS served in both houses of the Virginia Legislature, Secretary of the Interior, and Rector of the University of Virginia.

left home. I was much gratified to meet with Brother John and Lummie in Wythe. Indeed I feel very thankful that I was permitted to meet all my old friends once more, all of whom I fear I will never see again. After taking a sad farewell of my friends in Wytheville, I went directly to Charlottesville without an hour's delay anywhere. There I stayed a day and two nights, spending my time very pleasantly indeed in company with Mr. Alexander's family, Misses Jones (sisters of Lieutenant Jones our instructor) and Misses Gilmer (cousins of ours, daughters of the lamented Mrs. W. Gilmer). One of the Misses Jones will pay a visit to the Point in the course of a week. I shall be very happy to see her. After leaving Charlottesville I reached Richmond in about five hours, about ten minutes after my friend John Pegram had left for the Point. I regretted this very much but Mrs. Pegram said I could not regret it more than he did, and that he would not have left but for the fact that the Roanoke steamship on which he wished to take passage did not sail again for a week. I can never forget Mrs. Pegram's kindness to me while at her house. Miss Pegram was as lovely as ever. We had a great laugh over the sleep. Miss Pegram walks a mile or two every morning before breakfast. I became acquainted with Mrs. Caskie[122] (Mrs. Pegram's sister) who is a charming woman, as well as several others with whom I became acquainted. I stayed with Mrs. Pegram a day and a half and wished very much that it could have been a month. From Richmond I came straight to New York. I spent my time very usefully here visiting the different parts of the city, and met with nearly all my companions in arms of their way to the Point, Pegram among others. My associates seemed to enjoy themselves very much visiting theatres and other like places of amusement, but I no doubt enjoyed myself equally well in other more instructive pursuits. Next day we came up on the "Reindeer" and landed

---

[122] Francis Jane Johnston Caskie

amid the huzzas and salutations of the Corps. That night our Grand Ball came off during a violent storm of wind and rain, but notwithstanding the inclemency of the weather, I understand (as I did not attend) the large hall was densely crowded with ladies, leaving scarcely room to dance. The Point has been perfectly crowded with visitors all the summer so much so that the authorities were under the necessity of taking steps to render camp less attractive by tearing down the large awning in rear of the guard tent which sheltered them from the sun, besides several other prohibitory measures. We will soon be marshaled into the old routine of duty, and then for two more years we are afloat. I am quite well. I could not conveniently obtain more than two daguerreotypes and as I had a good opportunity I sent them to Brother Alex and to another whom I had promised one in Wytheville. I will bring you one as well as Vic and Lummie when I return. Don't forget to send me yours. My love to Vic and Buz and tell Vic to write.

      Your affectionate son,
      J. E. B. Stuart

TO BETTIE HAIRSTON[123]

  United States Military Academy, West Point, New York
  September 23, 1852

My Dear Cousin,

  I trust that the anxiety I have felt to know how my friends at Beaver Creek[124] have been getting along since I saw them, as well as the sincere attachment I formed for them during our short acquaintance will serve as an apology for my want of ceremony in presuming to write to you. Indeed I have always thought that friendship and ceremony are

---

[123] Elizabeth Perkins (Bettie) Hairston (February 28, 1836-April 24, 1922)
[124] Beaver Creek Plantation in Martinsville, Henry County, Virginia.

completely antagonistic principles, that is: friendship in its pure unvitiated and unaffected form, which comes from the heart, and not the mere smile that glows with deception, which we too often meet with, in our intercourse with the world. By virtue of this distinction between true friendship and ceremonious friendship, I wish to show you to which class mine belongs, by trespassing on your attention, or rather patience, for a few moments.

   Since I parted with you, I have been kept busy traveling up to my arrival here on the 28th August; but I assure you no change of place or situation could prevent me, from often recurring to incidents connected with my visit to Beaver Creek, with the motions of purest delight; indeed every circumstance is now painted before me as vividly, as if it were but yesterday that I saw you. The 'blackberry hunt' the walk over the to the spring, my exploit on the water gap, our frequent excursions in the garden, the old hen catching lightning bugs, the harvesters' serenade, and above all your own delightful performance on the Piano, which I was rascal enough to enjoy without your consent, all revive in my heart unfading recollections of the joy I experienced during that visit. I will never forget it. The gourd which you were so kind as to give me I carried from Beaver Creek home in my hand, and thence brought it in my trunk to this place, and it is now hanging before me in a very conspicuous part of our room, which has in consequence become the resort of all the southerners, for the luxury of drinking out of an "old Virginny gourd". I have cut on the out side "Bettie" which excites their curiosity very much; they are anxious to know who "Bettie" can be, and the only way to satisfy them is to come to the Point next summer so as to give them a practical illustration of what "Bettie" is. If you come I promise to have my gourd ready to offer you a drink. The world's Fair will be going on about the same time.[125] I enjoyed myself exceedingly during the whole of my furlough, and at its close had only to regret that it was so short. Upon arriving at home, after my trip to Henry and Pittsylvania. I received a letter from Sister Mary[126] (Brother A's wife) informing me of the precarious state of her health and of her intention to set out for the Scott Springs forthwith, which determined me to set out for the latter place very soon, this trip took up the remainder of my furlough.[127] I found her in a state of rapid convalescence, and as I have heard nothing to the contrary since, I hope she has by this time entirely recovered. I feel for her the same attachment as if she were a sister. It would have afforded me the greatest pleasure to have been able to pay you a visit at the Springs, for I know we could have had so much fun rambling over those cliffs, gliding in our canoes along the river, and encountering the Lucas', on Salt Pond, but you can appreciate my hurry when I tell you that I did not stay more than 10 days in all at home.[128] I have no doubt that you enjoyed your trip especially if Ruf French contributed his usual fund of merriment on the occasion. I suppose of course he visited you.

In order to form anything like a true idea of the appearance of West Point you must see it; to describe its grand and picturesque mountain scenery its noble river and beautiful Plain, is what has often been attempted by far abler pens than mine without success. To say the least, it is well worth a trip from Virginia here to see approaching and retiring along north River, you proceed up the river for about 20 miles your eyes feasting all the while on the lovely prospect that spreads before you on either side, with here and there a magnificent country seat, lifting its huge dome into the sunshine, which a group of towering elms excludes from below. Among the most prominent of these are the

---

[125] The Crystal Palace Exposition in New York City in 1853.
[126] Mary Carter Stuart (1831-1862), wife of William A. Stuart.
[127] JEBS brother WAS and his first wife Mary Taylor Carter.
[128] Salt Pond in Giles County, Virginia.

princely dwelling of Forrest the Tragedian, and the more plain, but no less elegant mansion of Washington Irving.[129] The former especially is, comparatively speaking, quite a palace. To gaze upon the broad expanse of pleasure grounds parks and gardens, which environ it with true oriental style, and the myriads of flowers, which team forth on every avenue, laughing with joy, and their imagine the incessant warble of the winged songsters that must frequent so sweet a place, any person without information to the contrary, would pronounce Edwin Forrest the happiest of mortals. The residence of Irving seems to accord perfectly with the predominant characteristic of his immortal productions, elegant simplicity.

    Leaving this scene of beauty you find your view suddenly confined by the palisades, which consist of an immense barrier of solid rock extending for several miles along the river on your left, rising in unique grandeur to the clouds. On your right a range of barren ridges gradually swell, as the recede into mountains. Passing along you find yourself suddenly in the midst of the romantic scenery of the Highlands. After doubling one of these cliffs which jutting forth into the river, stands like a sentinel, and in superstitious days no doubt seemed to eye with marked vigilance every craft that trespassed on its protégé, there opens upon your view a scene of ideal beauty. Your eyes now rest upon West Point. Its broad plain about 150 feet above the river, surrounded by high mountains, its beautiful buildings, magnificent Barracks, the proud banner floating gracefully from a conspicuous point, the white mountains that modestly peer forth from the numerous cedar groves are well calculated to invest the place with more than ordinary interest. But land here, and spend a few hours by way of gratifying the little curiosity

---

[129] Washington Irving's home, Sunnyside, was in Tarrytown. Edwin Forrest's home, Fonthill Castle, was in the Hudson Valley of New York.

which its first appearance may have excited, and accompany your cousin in a survey of the Point.

After visiting all the scenes of interest the Barracks the different galleries of paintings, sculpture, trophies, minerals and we go out to the Battalion drill. Here are all the Cadets in different capacities executing exactly the same maneuvers which would be performed on the battlefield, the impetuous charge with bristling bayonets, the hurried retreat, as well as the fierce fire, all done with a symmetry so perfect as to be really surprising to a stranger to such things. Having tired ourselves gazing on the mock battles, and had our ears almost deafened by the uproar of artillery, and also seen "Tony" perform in a charge of cavalry, we will walk up to Fort Putnam which is situated on an eminence far above and immediately in rear of the plain. You know that this was the spot, on which, at one time, rested the fate of our Republic. It was Washington grand reserve on which to rally his dearest {illegible}, and with reason, for it has withstood alike the assaults of treason and the inroads of time. Standing on its hoary ramparts you feel as if you were treading on sacred ground; indeed it is hallowed by the most thrilling associations. Around you are the rude remains of entrenchments, while immediately under you is a gloomy cell lighted by a porthole through which was echoed thunder in the Revolution! Lifting your eyes from objects immediately around you, you are greeted by a scene surpassing in loveliness and magnificence the loveliest conception of fancy. Far below lies West Point standing forth in grand relief from the Hudson whose majestic wave is gliding on to the ocean. Upon its placid bosom softly glide numerous sloops, whitening its dark course, as far as the eye can reach; unchecked by the current, in deathlike stillness, they quietly await the propitious breeze as it skims over the deep, to waft them to their far-off destination. As you are no doubt tired of all this tirade, without being so ungallant as to leave you to share the cold comfort of Fort Putnam, I will escort you back to the Hotel and after seeing you comfortably lodged, end my description.

The usual Ball come off on the 28th of August and such an assemblage of beauty fashion and gaiety I never say before. Notwithstanding the violent storm, which raged without all night, the Hall was crowded with ladies and continued so till 12. The music was charming and the whole scene within presented a singular contrast to the storm without. Although the music and the busy whirl of the dance succeeded in drowning the rain, yet the thunder gave unmistakable evidence of its existence by the successive peals that roared from above every noise. With many a long face we marched into Barracks next day to resume the arduous duties of another year, which have kept us so busy that we have had time scarcely to turn around. I have employed a little leisure to day in giving you this hasty scrawl relying upon your generosity to overlook and pardon every error, and at the same time hoping that I will not witness the advent of many mails without a letter from Cousin Bettie. Although our acquaintance was so short still I desire to be remembered in love to Aunt Ann, Uncle Marshall, Cousins Henry and Ann, and always regarded by yourself.[130]

       As your affectionate Cousin
       J. E. B. Stuart

P. S. Please present my kindest regards to Miss Backus.[131]

---

[130] Marshall and Ann Hairston were the parents of Bettie and Ann Hairston.
[131] Miss Backus was Bettie Hairston's music teacher.

G. W. Custis Lee, J. E. B. Stuart and Stephen D. Lee circa 1854.

TO BETTIE HAIRSTON

      United States Military Academy, West Point, New York

      November 6, 1852

Dear Cousin Bettie,

      The fondly hoped for pleasure of hearing from you came at last; and I have only delayed expressing to you my grateful acknowledgements for such a distinguished favor in order if possible to gather material for a reply worthy of such an affectionate and entertaining letter. Nor can I promise you that my efforts, which (Pardon the egotism) I think have been quite praiseworthy, have been attended with success. For I imagine that there can be, in the monotonous routine of a soldier's life, little to interest one whose sources of pleasure I know to be so manifold and fruitful. I thought that to look on the trim and symmetrical form of Tony might inspire me with some noble thoughts but I found on coming to the test that I experienced such a childish impatience to mount him that sublime thought never entered the question. But if I fail to entertain, perchance you may [bestow] a smile on my folly, and if I fail in both I have the consolation that I did my best, and will rely on your own generosity which can, I know, never be deaf to such an appeal, to excuse the attempt.

      I was pleased to see that you remembered the little incidents connected with my visit to Beaver Creek with as much and indeed more vividness but certainly not more pleasure than myself. I had forgotten the scrape (or as I am a soldier I should have said "encounter") with the jar-fly until you reminded me. But now I distinctly remember every stratagem and maneuver of the onset, how when I was in the very act of surprising the enemy in his stronghold he gave me the slip, and particularly the good-natured rejoicing you and John evinced at my being foiled. That was but a simple illustration of the disappointments I experienced throughout my furlough. How often did I fancy that I had a pleasure within my grasp! But just before closing my fingers it took its flight just as the jar-fly. But in spite of these disappointments I had a glorious time.

Since I last wrote to you not only the fairy like beings who flitted over the Plain with a smile of deception enthroned on every lip, but even the green woods and grassy lawn have deserted us; and instead of the rich foliage we have the naked branches of huge elms rising spectre-like in relief against the sky, and for the soft and balmy breezes that fanned our cheeks on many a sultry evening after drill, there roars in rude contrast the chill nor-easter. Winter has already given us perceptible indications of his approach by sundry dispatches of his white winged messengers. The cold here during the winter is much severer than in Virginia, but this is a cold subject and enough to make you shiver to read about it, so with your permission we will turn to a brighter, as well as warmer theme, I allude to Giles.[132]

As I think I said before, I have regretted ever since that I was necessarily compelled to forego the great pleasure I anticipated on parting with you, of meeting you again amid the romantic scenery of Giles; but your glowing description of its beauties and your pleasant excursions on land and water have alone brought me fully to realize how much I lost. Yet when I come to reflect seriously on the matter, it looks like greediness to want all the pleasure, but it is human nature; the Poet says,

"Man wants but little here below,

Nor wants that little long"[133]

---

[132] Giles County, Virginia.
[133] Lines from Oliver Goldsmith's *The Hermit*.

Though I think however little that may be, he is never satisfied with it; and true to this principle in our nature, not satisfied with the enjoyment which Beaver Creek afforded me, I really envy the barren hills and ragged cliffs of Giles your company, however rude subjects for envy you may consider them. (This sentence is so ambiguous that I wish I could erase it but I trust to you to put on the construction intended.)

In Dear old Virginia October and November I consider by far the most delightful months of the year, and nothing would please me better than to be able to try some of your fine grapes and delicious water to day, as well as to see some of your beautiful flowers of which you know I am so fond. I well remember how lovely looked the sweet Cape Jessamine that bloomed in the Arbor, as also how I got my finger stuck prying into the affairs of the mocking bird. By the way you ought to see with what care I have preserved the little rose and piece of arbor vitae, which you gave me in the garden; if you could I think you would be constrained to reward me with another.

The election which absorbs the attention of all has failed to create any enthusiasm in the corps and has elicited scarcely any notice except a little idle curiosity on the part of some to see the returns, just like the indifferent inquiry usually after a fight "which whipped". The General was here a few weeks ago and I understand was quite sanguine. We greeted him with the usual Salute. Miss Ella Scott and her mother have honored us with their company for several months. It is said that Mrs. Gen[eral] Scott is strong for Pierce.[134]

I am very well pleased with West Point for the limited stay which I expect to make but so long as your kind letters remind me that there is such a bright spot as Virginia I can never be content to take up

---

[134] Franklin Pierce was the fourteenth president of the United States and had served under General Winfield Scott during the Mexican War.

my abode here permanently. If it could be granted on Virginia soil I would consider it a paradise. I am sorry that my friends will not have the exquisite pleasure of knowing who "Bettie" is next summer, though I sincerely hope that you will not fail to show them before we leave the Point. I congratulate you upon escaping the Lucas though no doubt if you had encountered one you would have given him a reception, which he would have remembered. If the Misses Jones visited West Point I did not know it; I hope you will not suffer any of your friends to visit New York without coming here nor coming here without making themselves known to me. I am as glad to see any Virginian as if he were an old acquaintance.

I think "Love not" is beautiful, though I think my decision is based on admiring the music, rather than endorsing the sentiment.[135] It is played delightfully by our Band, though I have no doubt I will be still more charmed to hear it on your piano if I should ever enjoy that pleasure.

Present my compliments to Miss B. and give my best love to Uncle Marshall, Aunt Ann, and Cousin Ann, Ruth and Jack. I hope the latter has recovered and trust that he will be able to commit considerable havoc among the walnuts this season. Tell Cousin Ruth I continue to look forward with pleasure to time when she will let me not only see but wear her crotchet hat. In conclusion allow me to express the hope that I will be favored by another letter so kind and entertaining as your former one. I have just drunk your health from the gourd and send you a piece of arbor vitae, which I plucked from the brink of Hudson as a slight token of the regard of

Your affectionate Cousin
J. E. B. Stuart

---

[135] *Love Not* with lyrics by Caroline Norton and music by John Blockley.

P. S. I am happy to see from a letter, which I received yesterday from sister Mary Stuart, that her health is good, and that my other sister Mary is likewise enjoying comparatively good health.[136]

TO BETTIE HAIRSTON

      United States Military Academy, West Point, New York
      December 20, 1852

Dear Cousin Bettie,

      After waiting long and anxiously for an answer to my last letter I concluded that I must have failed to reach you, and resolved to write again to find out its fate. But just as I was upon the point of putting my resolve in execution, your kind and interesting favor of Nov[ember] 30th arrived. Its perusal sufficed to make me forget every shadow of blame, which I before imagined ought to be, imputed to you for so long a delay. Besides on examining the dates I found that your letter was exactly two weeks on the road whereas it should have been only 6 days. Where do our letters stop? Don't you think Cousin Bettie that we ought to complain to the Post Office Department? But without joking I must confess that however the case may be with you, I would much rather they would not delay the pleasure which your welcome letters always afford me, by keeping them so long on the road. I think that either the Post boy got a duckling, or the stage capsized in a mud hole, which was honored with the transportation of your last letter; for it came to me bearing unmistakable evidences of where mud had been; but I assure you it was none the less acceptable on that account. The thoughts, which its language breathed, were as dear to me as if they had been inscribed in gold.

---

[136] First reference is to J. E. B. Stuart's sister-in-law Mary Taylor Carter Stuart and second is to sister Mary Tucker Stuart.

You say Miss B. has left you that her full-orbed moons have left their accustomed orbits no more to beam with radiant light upon Beaver Creek Academy. Although my best wishes will ever attend that lady in all her peregrinations round the world, yet I must say in simple justice to her that she possessed a peculiar kind of elasticity in her musical performance, a kind of jumping motion which I could not admire and which I would not have you to imbibe with her other musical teaching for the world. I regret to learn that her sister's health was such as to suspend her operations at Cousin George's.[137] I became slightly acquainted with her on my return, and suppose it is needless to say that I was better pleased with her than her sister. You are very anxious for some deep snow. If you will pay us a visit this winter I promise to supply you a plenty of it, and give you some delightful sleigh-rides, as well as a plenty of ice to skate upon if you desire it. These Yankee Girls are very fond of skating. I don't know when I have been more surprised than when one morning during the first winter of my Cadet-ship. I saw from my window one of the Professor's daughter gliding on a pair of skates "like a thing of beauty". But I soon learned from those more versed in "yankee tricks" that in north and Vermont especially skating constituted the Ladies' principal amusement. Don't you think you would like it? But my space is too precious for me to waste with a dissertation on Yankee Customs. Let us go back to Dear old Virginia.

    I reckon Cousin George's wife has not yet forgotten my unceremonious call that stormy night about 10 or 11 o'clock. Next morning I was astonished to see through what a complication of lanes gates and fences I had found my way the night before which was certainly the darkest I ever saw. I did not however reach the house until I

---

[137] George Stovall Hairston (1813-1854) of Greenwood, Henry County, Virginia.

had knocked the yard-gate down. I believe Cousin Matilda (I believe that is Cousin George's wife's name) had a design on my gourd for next morning when I was ready to start it was missing, and when I concluded to stay a little longer the gourd again made a very miraculous disappearance. But I was not to be cut out of Cousin Bettie's nice present in that manner, and when I called for it again, she laughed a good deal saying that she intended telling you about my tenacity to the gourd. If she ever do, please ask her to tell the part she acted in the play. I liked her and Cousin George very much indeed and regretted exceedingly that I could not stay with them longer. I intended spending the next day at Cousin Tyler's[138], but they arrived (I mean Cousin Tyler and Pocahontas) at Cousin George's next morning before I left on their way to Cousin Louisa's.[139] I thought it would not do to turn them back, so I told them I could not stop.

The weather tonight is dreadfully cold, and the wind howls so mournfully through our halls that if I were not answering Cousin Bettie's sweet letter I would be liable to an attack of the "Blues". The only thought that makes me sad is that so long a time must elapse before I can see you all again, that so many months, which spent among my friends in Virginia, would seem hours, of military duty must intervene ere I land on old Virginia soil. I have had recourse to the inspiration of Tony but I think by the time you finish this letter you will agree with me that his inspiration availed as little as it did in my former letter.

I am a thousand times obliged to you for the beautiful rose and sprig of Arbor vitae which your letter contained. I will prize it dearly as a token of your regard hoping that I may never prove myself unworthy of

---

[138] John Tyler Hairston (1811-1858) of Marrowbone, Henry County, Virginia, married Pocahontas Rebecca Cabell.
[139] Louisa Hardyman married George Hairston (1784-1863) and lived at Marrowbone, Henry County, Virginia.

it. I enclose you a sprig Arbor vitae which I plucked on the bank of the Hudson near Flirtation Walk; please accept it as a testimonial of that deep and lasting regard I feel for you, and of which nothing as frail as a flower can convey an adequate idea.

Soon after writing to you last I received the melancholy news of the death of my Uncle Judge Brown, which was a source of deep regret. In him I have lost my best friend and the community its noblest ornament.[140] I believe I can never realize that he has gone until I return to his hospitable roof and find him no longer there to welcome me. This world, Cousin Bettie, contains so few true friends that you will pardon me for paying the slight tribute to one long tried and true.

A few weeks ago we had a delightful visitor here in the person of Miss Eliza Meene of Lynchburg, Virginia with whom I became acquainted while on furlough. If you knew what a treat it is to me to meet with a Virginian, especially an old acquaintance and a lady you could imagine how much I enjoyed the charming society of Miss Meene and how I suffered with the Blues after her departure. I consider her visit as evidence that all Virginians do not forget us poor boys at West Point, and shall ever recur to it with emotions of pleasure as a bright spot on this winter's waste.

I would be most happy to spend this Christmas at Beaver Creek, but as I must forego that pleasure I must content myself with the thought or rather hope that I will be remembered in the gay circle that gathers around your Christmas fire. I heard from my sister Mary of Wythe only a few days ago; she had a slight cold but was in other respects well.[141] I have not had the pleasure of receiving a letter from Vic[toria] since her return to Salem but trust I will soon.[142]

---

[140] James Ewell Brown of Wythe County, Virginia was the second husband of Anne Dabney Stuart, the sister of Archibald Stuart, father of JEBS.
[141] JEBS sister-in-law Mary Stuart, who lived in Wythe County, Virginia

Give my best to Uncle Marshall, Aunt Ann, Cousins Ann, Ruth and Jack. Tell Cousin Ruth I thank her for her kind advice and will try to follow it, but in the mean time must beg leave to inquire after the "crotchet hat". I hope I will have the pleasure of wearing it when I return to Virginia in [18]54. Please let my hear from you soon and with the sincere hope that you may have a merry Christmas and a happy new year and also that while I am penning this your slumbers may be attended with dreams of happiness that will not be "all a dream". I bid you a good night.

J. E. B. Stuart

Dec[ember] 25th This letter has been accidentally detained until today. Christmas gift.[143]

TO MISS HELEN ALEXANDER

West Point, New York

January 6, 1853

Cadet Stuart presents his kindest regards and sincere thanks to Miss Alexander for the lovely bouquet and slippers which she was pleased to send him, and begs leave to assure her that the pleasant moments spent with her are still cherished by him among the sweetest reminiscences of furlough. The beautiful slippers are worthy of a more honored place that the one to which she consigned them, yet he indulges the hope that he may never prove himself unworthy of her regard, and will always deem it a high privilege to be able to call Miss Helen his <u>friend.</u>

---

[142] JEBS sister Victoria was attending Salem Academy, a female school in Salem, North Carolina.

[143] Judge Peter Hairston of Cooleemee states in his editing of this letter in the North Carolina Historical Review that is was a tradition on plantations to give a Christmas gift to slaves who quoted this phrase.

Miss Helen, I leave etiquette on the other page and turn over to have a "tete a tete" with you. A sweet cousin of mine in Richmond at school writes to me that her brother Mr. Pannill of the University has been so fortunate as to form your acquaintance. I was truly happy to hear that he had fallen in such good hands. I commit him to your keeping. I am waiting anxiously to welcome you on West Point next June. I have told Mr. A. to present my <u>regards</u> to the ladies but I commission you to give my <u>love</u> to them all. Particularly to the Misses Jones for whom I feel a partiality in gratitude for their visit.

You say you have "taken the privilege of making me the slippers", I assure you I desire no greater privilege than that of accepting them. With the sincere wish that they year on which you have just entered may preserve your heart as unclouded as a summer's sky

                        I am Miss Helen
                        Sincerely your friend
                        J. E. B. Stuart

Above, Beaver Creek and below, Marrowbone, both homes of the Hairstons in Henry County, Virginia.

TO BETTIE HAIRSTON

West Point, New York, March 23, 1853

Cousin Bettie,

I wrote a letter to Vic[toria] last week in which I communicated to you what I conceived to be a reasonable apology for my long delay.[144] The privation to you was no doubt trifling but the pleasure it would have afforded me was so great that it is still a source of deep regret. As you requested that I would write to you as soon as you arrived at Salem. I would have been willing to have made any sacrifice to have done it. But if I had complied with your wishes, such would have been the hurry absolutely necessary to make, that I would have been farther than ever from doing you the justice which your estimable letters demand. My excuse is that usually rendered by the Schoolboy, want of time, but there is this difference, my want of time was not occasioned by an unwonted pressure of study, as is usually the case with other School boys, for I assure you my fondness for the occult principles, and learned researches in Science is never so great as to prevent me from laying my Astronomy on the shelf and proceeding to the unfeigned pleasure of having a talk with Cousin Bettie. My want of time was owing to the preparation of "Muster rolls" which are required from each company every two months, and the duty of preparing them devolves upon the First Sergeants; also the preparation of a speech for an Exhibition of the Dialectic Society, neither of which was it possible for me to avoid.[145]

Once more Spring has returned. The Point has already assumed a more life-like aspect. This is a lovely morning. I wish so much Cousin that you could have been here at parade this morning. All nature seemed to wear a charm. The martial strains of music once more enlivened the

---

[144] JEBS sister Victoria Augusta Stuart
[145] The Dialectic and Amosophic were debating societies at the USMA.

plain imparting elasticity to every tread and infusing every heart with military ardor, while the Commanding voice of the major gave the Battalion quite a warlike appearance. The unruffled bosom of our beautiful river, as the last strains of music died away in the distance, sent up an echo of delight, while joyous Crownest from his sunny crest looked down with a smile of exultation.[146] Talk of the Italian Skies but if ever sun shown fairer or Sky looked purer than this morning it must have been superb in an infinite degree. A few evenings ago having a few moments leisure I was taking a quiet stroll on the side walk which Skirts the plain, absorbed in a train of alternate reflections and admiration of the magnificent prospect spread before me, when who must disturb my reverie but Miss B, who seemed to be actuated by the same motive as myself.[147] It is needless to add that I turned back with her and after reaching the end of the sidewalk we both came to the conclusion that it was better walking on Flirtation walk. And although we did not apply our walk in the way which its name would seem to indicate still I plucked her a piece of Arbor Vitae and she gave me three balls from her rigolette, which now adorn the column in my room not far [from] the dearly cherished Gourd.[148]

  I suppose you received the usual number of Valentines this year, for my part, I did not receive any, thus showing that after all my devotion to the Ladies during last summer they have forgotten me in so short a time. Such is the inconstancy of the Sex to which my Dear Cousin belongs. Well I reckon by this time your like myself are beginning to find out what a glorious place home is as compared with a monotonous boarding School. And I venture to say that when your eyes once more

---

[146] The Crow's Nest is the highest peak along the Hudson River.
[147] Miss was the daughter of Claudius Berard was the instructor of French at USMA from 1815 until 1848.
[148] A rigolette is a scarf worn on the head

rest on the beautiful trees and flowers of Beaver Creek, you will more than ever enjoy an evening walk to the black-berry patch, and doubly appreciate a gourd of water from that never-to be forgotten Spring. When that happy time arrives mine will be the regret that I can not share your pleasure, run races, pull flowers, eat green apples walk the log and try to catch locust with Cousin Bettie. Instead of that, I will be here, a poor soldier, serving my country, stalking up and down a sentinels post contemplating the new-born beauties of a midnight moon, and musing over the happy times of last summer still fresh in memory. But because I cannot share it, I do not on that account wish your enjoyment less, on the contrary I hope that Beaver Creek has never looked more lovely nor hours glided so sweetly as they will to you next summer. And I will consider myself highly favored if you write to me then { }

I am pained to inform you that Tony was {}. He was condemned by a board of officers as being {} nently had to suffer the penalty. Was it not {} his valuable services by such treatment? But there is consolation in the thought that such is the "Fortune of war" and we are all victims ready for sacrifice {} when it shall please U. S. I propose therefore that we wear mourning on the little finger for one week. His loss I deeply deplore. I suppose I will have to content myself with Duroc, Bembo, Roderick or Don Quixote or Forager, or Jerry. Which do you prefer?

We expect to have an immense crowd of visitors here during the ensuing encampment. All the rooms at our two large Hotels are engaged, which has never been done so early before.[149] The World's Fair will attract an immense number. I indulge the hope that among the number I shall be able to identify an old friend or two.

---

[149] The West Point Hotel was located near Trophy Point was government owned. It was known as Cozzen's, but as Roe's during JEBS time at the USMA

What has become of Cousin Peter and Lummie. I have not heard from them in Six months. I suppose like a good Democrat you are giving your hearty support to the administration of Gen[eral] Pierce. By the way did you ever see in the Examiner an article about our Superintendent?[150] You must excuse my lack of interest this time, I trust however that as glorious spring advances and those "birds of passage" the Ladies who took their flight at the first approach of winter, begin to return, that I will be able to tell you something that will make you laugh. Have you any Spiritual Rappers or Bloomers at Salem?[151] If not we are that much ahead of you. Please give my love to Vic and my Cousins and write soon to.

Your devoted
{Signature Missing}

TO ARCHIBALD STUART

West Point, New York, April 5, 1853

Dear Pa,

I received your kind letter last week and was gratified to learn that you still enjoyed good health. For my part, I never enjoyed better health in my life than I have enjoyed ever since I returned from furlough. Our spring drills have begun and now we have less time than ever for recreation, but the Plain has already begun to assume the robe of beauty, and everything in nature teams with life and joy, I hope that General [President] Pierce in his liberal extension of privileges and immunities of faithful Democrats will not forget to give you an opportunity of seeing

---

[150] Robert E. Lee became the ninth superintendent at the USMA on September 1, 1852. The Richmond Examiner was edited by John M. Daniel from 1847 until 1854.

[151] Spiritual Rappers supposedly communicated with the dead. Bloomers were trousers similar to female dresses.

what a paradise we have here. The appointments of Visitors for next June have been already made by Mr. Fillmore, and as the states alternate annually, Virginia will not have a Visitor here until June after next when I graduate should I be blessed with that good fortune. I think Mr. Pierce will be apt to appoint some old companion in Congress; but "nous verrons". I think Mr. Fillmore acted strangely about the matter. The appointment strictly belonged to Mr. Pierce. Mr. Fillmore, also not satisfied with filling the vacancy occurring next June. He might as well have appointed a judge in the event that Mr. Cushing should be one of the Cabinet. But you have enough of politics in the Senate. I sent an article to the Examiner which appeared in Friday's number over the signature "S". So you perceive I begin to figure in the columns of newspapers. Have you never seen Mrs. Pegram? What has become of Cousin Sue? Remember me kindly to Doctors Watson and Headen, Messrs. Hairston, Price {Thomas R.) Parker, Boyd and all other friends. Please write again before you adjourn and believe me still

       Your affectionate son, Jim

TO BETTIE HAIRSTON

  United States Military Academy, West Point, New York
  May 7, 1853

My Dear Cousin,

  The pleasure, which your sweet letter afforded me, can only be equaled by the reception of another. I was truly glad to learn that you had become duly initiated into the routine of duty at Salem without the dissatisfaction and depression of spirits usually experienced by those who resign the gentler influences and sweeter joys of a quiet though lovely home for the noise, confinement, and restraint of a boarding school. I had considerable confidence in your capability of self-denial, and disposition to bear things like a philosopher, but you outreached my estimate when you stood your ground so well as at Salem. Although every one deems his own home

"A spot supremely blest,

A dearer, sweeter Spot than all the rest,"[152]

Yet experience has taught me that it is necessary to be deprived of it awhile in order to appreciate it properly. I might have rambled over the dear old hills of Patrick amid all pleasures of a mountain home for a life time without Drum Head's appearing clothed with half that enchanting loveliness which greets my imagination when it recurs to it in contrast with "le champ militaire" of West Point.[153] And I think you will find the same the case with Beaver Creek. But do not understand me to undervalue the Point for I still consider it a magnificent spot, but so long as it remains in Yankee land, and so long as I cannot call it home, it cannot, in my estimation, begin to compare with that humble spot, Drum Head. Pardon me my Dear Cousin for such a tirade upon the charms of home with which you are doubtless, just now at least, more conversant than any one else.

Since my last letter our plain, mountains, and river have resumed the lovely drapery of summer and appear more beautiful than I ever saw them; I wish so much that you could see them, what delightful moonlight-strolls we would take round flirtation walk! And how gladly would we quaff from our never-to-be-forgotten gourd the classic water of Kosciusko's spring! But it is folly for me to indulge in such extravagant exclamations, for can I possible {} expect you to leave the charms of

---

[152] The West Indies Part 3 by James Montgomery "His home, the spot supremely blest A Dearer, sweeter spot than all the rest."
[153] Drum Head was the name associated with the site of a trial for the Tories that killed JEBS great-grandfather William Letcher in 1780.

Columbia Lafayette Stuart and her children.

home and the sweet society of "Old Folks at Home" to visit a place,[154] I care not if it be a paradise, in a remote corner of Yankee land, to see a scarcely remembered Cousin? By the way have you learned "Old Folks at Home", I consider it a beautiful song, and our band plays it delightfully. I intend to get it and several other pieces of my choice for you and Vic and send them by Cousin Peter who is, to my extreme delight, going to give us a call during the summer.

I anticipate quite a pleasant time with the ladies next Encampment. But the more I see of these Yankee girls the more thoroughly I am convinced of their inferiority in ever respect to our Virginia ladies; in beauty especially. I have not yet selected a successor to Tony; I think it quite probable that your preference will induce me to take Forager, though I will give them all a fair trial.[155]

About three weeks ago a party consisting of Mrs. Lee, 2 Misses Berard, Pegram, Powell and myself went on a sort of picnic to the top of Crow nest about 2 ½ miles distant.[156] Our walk was agreeable in every respect, so much so that the ladies are talking of going again. Unfortunately the day after our walk Mrs. Lee received the melancholy intelligence of the death of her mother. Mrs. Custis of Arlington, Virginia, the wife of the adopted son of Gen[eral] Washington.[157] She left immediately for Virginia and I am afraid that so great a bereavement will deprive us of the pleasure of her society next summer.

I join with you in your best wishes for the success of Democracy, experience has fully demonstrated that its principles are the

---

[154] Old Folks Home was a song by Stephen Foster published in 1852.
[155] Tony and Forager were horses used by the Cadets at the USMA.
[156] Mrs. Robert E. Lee, the daughters of the late Claudius Berard, John Pegram and John G. Powell of Mississippi, the latter admitted in 1850, but did not graduate.
[157] Mrs. George Washington Parke Custis died in April 1853 and was the mother of Mary Lee, wife of Superintendent Robert E. Lee.

only ones, which will secure the permanency of our government and preserve the constitution and the rights of the states inviolate. While on the subject of politics I can't help expressing my deep regret at Dr. Averett's failing to be the Democratic nominee for our district. Bocock may be an abler man but he can't possibly be a more faithful representative. In the Convention I noticed that part of the Patrick Delegation voted for Bocock, I fell ashamed of such ingratitude towards a man who did for her what no other ever did; it gave her a representative at this Institution.[158]

The first of June the day, which is to put a temporary stop to study for both of us, is fast approaching, and will no doubt be here before I have the pleasure of hearing from you again. I will greet that day with rejoicing for ten months toils among "The abstruse regions of the philosophic {} world" recreation is by no means unwelcome.[159] Play is more agreeable than work at all times.

You remarked that you saw in a number of the Examiner a communication which said that 5 Virginians would graduate and. did you suspect that your Cousin was the writer? How do you like Daniel's cutting editorials? He had a very amusing one last week about Col[onel] Boyd, which I suppose you saw. If you see any more communications in it from West Point you may consider me the author. I hope that while you are Beaver Creek I shall hear from you more frequently than during your stay at Salem. But for the new organization of the P. O. department I would fear that Post Masters would conspire against us again. It is to be hoped however that the day will come when a correspondence will be unnecessary. And when I think of your so soon treading the walks we

---

[158] Thomas Hamlet Averett was defeated for the Democratic nomination by Thomas Stanhope Bocock (1815-1891) for the seat in the U. S. House of Representatives.
[159] "abstruse" means difficult to understand or obscure.

once trod together I can but reiterate my regret that I cannot be with you. But I assure you if I am ever permitted to visit the Old Dominion again Beaver Creek will be on the first places to which I will repair.

A few days ago I had a visit from an old friend and neighbor Jonathon Carter now a Lieutenant in the Navy on the eve of starting out in Ringgold's expedition to Behrings Sts to be absent four years.[160] He looked better than I ever saw him and seemed to anticipate a fine time.

I wish you would write to me before leaving Salem. I have heard from Ma since her return, but have not yet received Vic's long expected letter. Give me love to her and all my Cousins at Salem. Remember me affectionately to all at Beaver Creek when you return, while I remain

Your devoted Cousin, J. E. B. Stuart

These two lines not meant to be sage
Were put here to fill out the page

TO ALEXANDER HUGH HOLMES STUART
United States Military Academy, West Point, New York
May 30, 1853
Dear Cousin,

Your kind letter enclosing me $100.00 was received today. I enclose you the receipt with my signature. Supposing from your delay that you had not received my first letter, I was induced to write a second which you have no doubt ere this received. From the few election returns which I have seen I should judge that your party has met with but little success in Virginia, but it does not become a military man to discuss politics. We look forward to the encampment which is now only a few

---

[160] Cadwalader Ringgold (1802-1867) led an expedition of five ships beginning in 1853 to survey the western Pacific. Captain Jonathan Hanby Carter (1821-1884) served in the United States and Confederate States' navies.

weeks off as a source of very great pleasure. The Point will no doubt be overrun with visitors from all parts of the Union. I am happy to say that at last I have the prospect of seeing some of my relatives here for Mr. Hairston and his lady (my sister) write me that they will certainly come. The Hippodrome is still drawing crowded audiences. I have heard many and varied accounts of it. Some call it a humbug while others (these constitute the majority) say it is well worth seeing, but be the truth as it may I am pretty certain that I will never have an opportunity of testing it. Give my love to Cousin Fanny, Augusta and Baldwin and believe me ever

       Yours truly, J. E. B. Stuart

P. S. I shall be most happy to hear from you or Cousin Baldwin at all times.

TO BETTIE HAIRSTON

  Camp "Jefferson Davis," West Point, New York
  June 29, 1853

My Dear Cousin

  After many weeks of anxious expectations your most acceptable letter reached me a few days ago. After ten months arduous labor and confinement to Barracks there could tome have been nothing more welcome amid the military bustle and parade of the Encampment than a word from Cousin Bettie. As a matter of course I have often thought of the enjoyment you experienced on returning from your first separation from home and friends and pictured to myself even in the noisy tumult of Camp the pleasant hours you must be now spending at Beaver Creek. Although I rejoice to think that your pleasures are so many still I must confess that my joy is mingled with the regret so often expressed that I cannot now have the exquisite pleasure of stealing softly to the door and lending an admiring ear to your performance of "Love Not" a sentiment so much oftener preached than practiced. I never admired Salem as an Institution but it is perhaps as good as any except those contaminated by abolitionism. I ask your pardon for introducing the subject but I do know that I have seen more misery in a limited sphere within the period of my sojourn north, than I ever dreamed of seeing, South, during my lifetime. This shows how perfectly absurd are all the outcries and attacks of Yankees against southern Institutions. They seem to forget that charity begins (where slander never does) at home.

You will observe that we have named our present Encampment in honor of our Sec[retar]y of War who is the first Graduate placed in the national cabinet.[161] The Encampment so far fully meets my expectations, that for which I most wished being granted in abundance that is, rest. The gay, fashionable season of Camp has not yet set in. It usually sets in on the 4th of July, but this year it will be much delayed on account of two very recent deaths in the Corps, which have cast a melancholy gloom over hearts lately teaming with joy. Since I came here these are the first of our number with whom disease has dealt fatally while here. They are Cadets Fort of N. Y. and Frank of Maine.[162] The former from consumption, the latter from congestion of the brain. The latter disease was brought on by mental anxiety in regard to the recent Examination, in which he ran the risk of being found deficient, and escaped only by fainting while undergoing his Examination which was followed by a serious attack which in the course of ten days brought a sad end to his life. But let us not dwell on so mournful a topic.

---

[161] Jefferson Davis (1808-1889) graduated from the USMA in 1828 and later became President of the Confederate States of America.

[162] James Edward Fort was admitted to the USMA in 1851 and died June 15, 1853; Charles W. Frank was admitted to the USMA in 1852 and died June 28, 1853.

Last Saturday I had the pleasure of dining at Col[onel] Lee's and found the Col[onel] in a fine humor. Mrs. Lee is still in Virginia, but we hope to see her again on the Point very soon. I have formed a high regard for the family. The garden was clothed in all {} its beauty and laden with the most delicious fruits reminding me forcibly of Beaver Creek, but the Cape Jessamine was wanting, and need I say there was wanting another flower which was my admiration at Beaver Creek, and so rare and lovely that I have never seen its equal anywhere else. I know not whether to call it the lily or the rose as the sweet purity of the one was beautifully blended in the beauties of the other. Indeed it seemed possessed of all the charms in appearance exhibited in the rich variety of tone of the lamented mocking bird to whose death you so feelingly and appropriately alluded. The name of the rare and beautiful flower if you do not know I will tell you some of these days when this frail letter shall have long lain in the depository of similar scribblings marked in Cousin Bettie's hand "To be forgotten". I assure you no one can imagine how anxious I will be to receive the welcome, which you in the name of my friends are pleased to promise me on my return.

I have become acquainted with a good many ladies so far and expect to mingle a good deal in their society during the present Encampment. When I meet with one who is kind hearted, fascinating and pretty it only serves by association of ideas to remind me of those I left in Virginia. If on the contrary I meet with one of the affected, fashionable, exquisite, flirts too often met with here, I am the more forcibly reminded by contrast of the superiority {} of our Virginia Girls. But at this particular time I wish so much that you were here to walk with me around "Flirtation" with whose beauties I have oftened {} endeavored, I fear in vain, to interest you. The breeze from the Hudson is so delightful, besides other attractions, which to me are irresistible. It is something funny that Flirtation walk ends where most flirtations seldom do at the church door.

Since we became First Classmen I have been promoted from 1st Serg[ean]t to Captain. So I will be "Captain Stuart" till I graduate provided my behavior is good enough. I enclose you a part of the insignia of my last office (orderly Sergeant) I would send all but there is not room in a letter. It is called a chevron, which is different for different offices and worn on each arm above the elbow. For instance for 1st Serg[ean]t it is "for Captain it is"

July 5th Yesterday was the great anniversary, as a {} of course Cadets were not at all wanting in evincing their {} proper display of the military. The procession {} my officers and the Corps fully equipped, moved in all the "pomp and circumstance of glorious war" to our capacious chapel our band leading the way flinging upon the greedy zephyrs the Soul-stirring air "Hail Columbia".[163] The orator of the day was Cadet Howard from Maine. The reader of the Declaration was, your cousin. Both were selected by the Dialectic Society. Howard's speech was a first rate one.[164] The audience was very large, for beside the Corps there congregated together samples of beauty and fashion from almost every part of the country except Virginia. I always thought I had enough brass, but when I rose before such an audience to perform the part assigned me I felt quite embarrassed, and would willingly have "crawfished" if it had been possible. But I had to "stand up to the rack fodder or no fodder", so I put on a bold face and drove ahead. After the affair was over we received the usual compliments and congratulations from our friends among the audience. We fired a national salute from our battery at 12m. The afternoon was devoted to recreation. Last night the

---

[163] Hail Columbia: Music by Philip Phile and words by Joseph Hopkinson.
[164] Oliver Otis Howard graduated in 1854 and served as a Major General in the U. S. Army during the Civil War.

first ball of the season came off contributing its usual share to the joy of the occasion. It lasted till 12. I went down as a spectator with some of my friends at the Hotel the Misses Murray of N. Y. who did not dance. They are excellent girls. One of them, Miss Ann embroidered a beautiful "S" on a pair of my gloves, which I will show you some of these days.

Give my best love to Uncle M. and Aunt Ann, also to Cousins Ann and Ruth and Jack. Lt. Sackett, our Instructor in Riding, is now absent buying horses, so I have not yet made my selection of a horse, nor will I until I see the result of his purchase.[165] It will be difficult to get so good a one as Toney. I beg you to answer me quickly. You cannot now plead the same excuse as at Salem.

{Close and Signature Missing}

TO BETTIE HAIRSTON

United States Military Academy, West Point, New York

August 17, 1853

Dear Cousin

Your interesting letter from Chapman Springs was duly received and would have been answered long ago but for the fact that you forgot to say when you expected to leave the Romantic beauties which then surrounded you for the more substantial comforts and pleasures of home. In that way you left me in doubt whether a letter sent forthwith to Giles would find you there. I concluded however that the surest course I could pursue was to wait quietly until the advance of the Season rendered it probable that you had left the mountains. Was I not right?

Sept[ember] 1st: Well Cousin Bettie the Gay and fashionable scenes that have for the last few months enveloped the Point like a work

---

[165] Lieutenant Delos B. Sackett of New York graduated from the USMA in 1845 and served as a Major General in the U. S. Army during the Civil War.

of magic have vanished. They have given place to the "sterner realities of a soldier's life" of which I have told you so much, but deep in our hearts are engraven images to remind us of the pretty faces and kind hearts that have by their society and sympathy softened hardship and fatigue into pastime. It would take a ream of foolscap to give a sketch of what has transpired since we enjoyed the glorious sleep and quiet in which my last letter left us, but as I have considerable partiality for my Cousin I will not trouble her with the perusal of quite so much. Our Cotillion parties coming off three times a week gave ample opportunity to those so inclined, to make the {} agreeable to our fair visitors. As a matter of course I did so. I formed many pleasant acquaintances and often wished that you could have been here to share them.

      I was on tiptoe for a long time in anticipation of the arrival of Ma, Lummy and Cousin P. They at length came, but it was only to stay from Saturday till Monday. Such a visit was really tantalizing, but I was too much gratified to see them, to think of complaining. Mrs. Pegram and Miss Mary have been here for two weeks but left us to day. Mrs. Lee and Miss Mary Lee also returned home some time since. Of the two Marys I admire Miss Mary Lee much the more, both as regards beauty and sprightliness. The latter has not appeared in company much since her Grand mother's death. But I must say that amid all the array of love-seekers and heart breakers by whom we have been surrounded, I have escaped unscathed. Whether my escape has been effected by my own generalship or whether Cupid regarded me as too unworthy a victim I leave your fancy to determine. And when I look around among my friends less fortunate than myself each with disconsolate look, musing absent-minded, by moonlight, clinging enthusiastically to the shattered and withered fragments of the last bouquet left him by this lady-love, and inditing sonnets to her eye-brows, I experience a good deal of silent satisfaction, and self-congratulation. They say that to be in love is a glorious predicament, but if it costs as much sleep as they lose in midnight communions with the stars and renders vacant seats in the Mess Hall as it seems to have done save me from such a monster. But I suppose you consider everything connected with the subject of love as nonsensical so I will drop the subject.

I have not heard a word from Virg[inia] since Ma and Cousin P. left I suppose they reached home safely or I would have heard something to the contrary. I became acquainted with Mr. P. H. Aylett and sister of V[irgini]a who were on a visit here some weeks ago.[166] You will find a letter from him while here in the Examiner of Aug[ust] 30th, which is decidedly the best and most correct of the kind which I have seen. You will pardon his partiality for the Institute when I tell you that he is one of the Board of Visitors to that Institution. He gave our friend Pegram a lift.

Sept[ember] 3rd: You see how often I have been interrupted {} since I began this by the recurrence of my daily duties, which must serve as an apology for the loose and disconnected manner in which this letter has been written. To day we ride. I have temporarily chosen Don Quixote, though I think it probable that I will take another.

I regret to learn of your anticipated departure for Miss[issippi] especially on account of the prevalence of yellow fever in that vicinity. I hope you will yet conclude not to leave the dear old Dominion but if you will go, I wish you a happy time, hoping that we will meet again at Beaver Creek next summer. Be assured the increased distance which will separate us will be far from lessening Cousin Bettie in my regard and I sincerely trust that associations of new friends and acquaintances will not

---

[166] Patrick Henry Aylett was an attorney in Richmond and a grandson of a Revolutionary statesman.

so far obliterate past ones as to cause her to forget to write frequently to "le soldat".

I have put away carefully the pretty spring of arbor vitae you sent me from Giles, for I prize it very highly because, coming from the highest crag it must have cost you a great deal of fatigue. I have not yet heard who is our judge. I suppose it will be Gilmer. Please write to me before you leave for Miss and tell me where you[r] all my dear Cousins. Lieut[enant] Cabell I suppose is now with you; look out for your heart it is said that epaulettes work like magic, and win more hearts than a Dictionary of honeyed words. I send you some pretty pieces of music played by the band here. I also send you Rayner's address, which I consider excellent.[167]

I am and hope to remain
Yours affectionately
J. E. B. Stuart

TO BETTIE HAIRSTON

United States Military Academy, West Point, New York
October 28, 1853

Dear Cousin Bettie,

I start this letter in answer to your welcome letter, before you get to Miss[issippi] in hopes that it may get there in time to welcome you to Yallabusha.[168] I assure you I duly appreciate the favor you bestowed by yielding to my benefit some of the last (and therefore precious) moments previous to your departure from the Dear Old Dominion. If you experience accords with mine while absent from Virginia, you will seize

---

[167] Kenneth Rayner of Hertford County, North Carolina, served in North Carolina and U. S. House of Representatives.
[168] The Yalobusha River in northeast Alabama flows into the Yazoo. The Hairston family owned estates in Lowndes County, Mississippi.

with avidity even the most trivial memorial of an absent friend. Such is the only claim, which this possesses for the perusal and flattering attention, which former ones have received at Cousin Bettie's hands. Knowing that the Yellow Fever was still raging with frightful havoc in Miss[issippi] and the South I hoped that regard fro your health would deter you from making the trip so soon, and since you have determined to do so, I confess I feel a little alarm (though you may laugh at it) in regard to the subject. But I will hope for the best, and look forward with pleasure to our meeting at Beaver Creek next Summer. What pleasant reminiscences the name recalls! My much-valued gourd that hangs on yonder hook has daily suggested to me some of the most delightful thoughts. I will endeavor to keep it as long as I live, for it will carry me back to Beaver Creek West Point and Bettie, subjects on which my mind will dwell with delight.

Just a week ago I was most agreeably surprised at the arrival of Dr. Headen and Sister Mary. And although they stayed only from Saturday till Monday I enjoyed their visit very much. A few days previous we had a visit from Mr. Broadnax (near Uncle Sam's), his daughter Miss Millie, Miss Jenny Ruffin and Mrs. Cameron her sister, with whom I had a very pleasant time.[169] Our honored "Alma Mater" Mrs. Gen[era]l Scott too has been on the Point for about a month, loading us as usual with her kind attentions. I received from her the other day a very kind note with a basket of grapes and which I wish you could have shared. I will preserve her letters among my "Distinguished Correspondence" of which unfortunately it is the only one on file. She claims all the Corps as her children, and is often asked by strangers if she

---

[169] Robert Brodnax of Woodlawn, Cascade, Virginia. Uncle Sam was Samuel Hairston of Oak Hill, the Hairston plantation in Pittsylvania County, Virginia. Anne Ruffin Cameron was the daughter of Chief Justice Thomas Ruffin and wife of Paul C. Cameron of Hillsborough, North Carolina.

has any sons to which she gives the invariable reply "250". I often tell Ma what indulgent a mother I have, and tell her there is great danger of being spoilt in which I fear is more truth than jest.

The Point at this time presents the most magnificent appearance I ever beheld. The fading leaves as they still linger reluctant to fall, are tinged with all the variegated hues of autumn. The weather is delightful and I can scarcely realize the fact that in a few weeks the plain will exhibit a picture of dreariness, which it makes me shiver to anticipate. And as you too will be very secluded in your retreat you will have abundance of time to devote to writing you will gratify your Cousin by writing as often as you can without inconvenience to yourself. My punctual answers will always testify my willingness to reciprocate in quantity if not in quality. And if you do not hear from me regularly take it for granted that I have written and the letter miscarried, and write to me.

Sister Mary and Doctor H[eaden] looked better than I ever saw them. The Doctor was engaged laying in his stock of Goods in the City. Both were perfectly delighted with the Point. My favorite wish now is for you and Vic[toria] to come on North next summer. I think we can prevail upon Doctor Stuart to spare a little time from his practice to be your escort, feeling confident that you two will be sufficient to take care of him.[170] The season of interest lasts from the first till the 20th of June inclusive and besides the real attractions of novelty and in such a tribute I am anxious before I leave to welcome you to West Point and show my friends who "Bettie" is. I hope cousin Bettie that you will not regard what I have said as prompted merely by politeness, but give it a favorable consideration proportionate to my anxiety to see you and make

---

[170] JEBS brother John Dabney Stuart practiced medicine in Floyd County, Virginia.

your calculations accordingly. It will only be a week or two's loss to Beaver Creek. All who have visited West Point from our section of country, in fact those too from all parts of the world, including those who have reveled in the Highland beauties of Scotland and basked in the pure sunlight of Italian skies, concur in pronouncing this the most lovely spot they ever beheld. So you see I am not alone in my partiality to the Point. You must be no means take my descriptions as fair representations of its beauties for they really surpass description. If it were only inhabited by warm-hearted Virginians and moved to our mountains I would never leave it.

  My home is fixed here for a while but after next June I have not the remotest idea what will become of me. If you are good at divining I wish you would try the art to determine my fate. Were I to consult my own inclinations at present I would continue in the army. It has attractions which to one who has seen a little of the "elephant" are overpowering. There is something in the "the pride and pomp and circumstance of glorious war", which makes "Othello's occupation" the most desirable of all.[171] Now tell me candidly had you not rather see your Cousin or even your brother a bold Dragoon than a petty-fogger lawyer. I have no doubt that you have a sort of partiality for the life of a farmer but that always pre-supposes the possession of a farm which you know is not always practicable so that the young man for whom capital has not already been accumulated is forced to adopt one of the hireling professions as Law Medicine Engineering and Arms. Between Law, Engineering and Arms I will choose before my leave expires next summer but as for Medicine; without meaning anything derogatory to my brother's taste, I must say that it is one which I can never be persuaded to. The officer has his toils but he has rewards. The lawyer has his cases

---

[171] Othello Act II, Scene 3, line 348 by William Shakespeare.

but seldom receives his fees. The physician has his patients and his sleepless nights but his patients are very patient in waiting to pay him. The Engineer must first have a reputation before he can get desirable employment. But you are no doubt tired of my dissertation on a choice of professions, I will relieve you passing to a different theme.

You say "Little Pete" expects to succeed me.[172] I am very glad indeed to hear it and hope that his expectations will be realized. I do not know him but I know his brothers Sam and George.[173] I saw one at Beaver Creek. You must tell me when you write how you found all our friends in Western Virginia, for I haven't heard from them in a month of Sundays. I reckon Jack will be killing ducks all the winter. I wish I could help him. I suppose you have no piano at your home in Miss[issippi]. You must miss such a companion to lonely hours, very much. I have some very pretty pieces, which I have been intending to send to you but I suppose it will be best now to wait until you return to Virginia unless you have a piano in Mississippi. There are several cadets from my class from Mississippi, Davis of Aberdeen, whom we call by the unpoetic name of "Gorgeous" and Mullins from the northern part.[174] The Instructor of Infantry Tactics of my company, Lieut[enant] Wilcox is a brother of a Congressman from Mississippi.[175] So your adopted state is not unrepresented.

You have never told me with what success Cousin Ruth met in her hat undertaking, I take it for granted however that she triumphed

---

[172] Peter Hairston (1835-1914) of Irvin, Henry County, Virginia entered USMA in 1854, but resigned to serve in the Civil War rising to the rank of colonel in the Confederate army.
[173] Samuel Hairston and George Isham Hairston of Henry County, Virginia.
[174] Benjamin Franklin Davis was killed at Brandy Station in June 1863. John Mullins born in Tennessee and appointed from Mississippi graduate in 1854.
[175] Cadimus M. Wilcox graduated USMA in 1846 and served as a general in the Confederate army. John A. Wilcox served as a Union Whig from Mississippi in the U. S. House of Representatives.

nobly. Do you ever attempt such things? Tell Cousin Ann I hope to have the pleasure of hearing her speak (a pleasure which I never had) when we meet next Summer. Remember me affectionately to all and write as soon as you can to

>Your Devoted Cousin
>J. E. B. Stuart

TO ARCHIBALD STUART (Undated 1854?)

I have not as yet any fixed course determined upon after graduation; still I can't help but regard it as the important crisis of my life. Two courses will be left for my adoption, the profession of arms and that of law; the one securing an ample support, with a life of hardship and uncertainty,--laurels, if any, dearly bought, and leaving an empty title as a bequeathment; the other an overcrowded thoroughfare, which may or may not yield a support, -- may possibly secure honors, but of doubtful worth. Each has its labors and its rewards. In making the selection I will rely upon the guidance of Him whose judgment cannot err, for "it is not with man that walk-eth to direct his steps."

(Fragment from *The Life and Campaigns of J. E. B. Stuart* by H. B. McClellan.)

TO BETTIE HAIRSTON
>United States Military Academy, West Point, New York
>February 9, 1854

Cousin Bettie,

My last letter to you was dated the 9th of December. Weeks gradually glided away, and I flattered myself with the prospect of soon receiving another your interesting and most welcome letters, but soon weeks grew into months and still no letter, such was my predicament which I in mediating upon to night suddenly remembered that I had promises if no answer came to my letters within a reasonable time to take it for granted that you had written and the letter miscarried and write again. So I hasten to repair so great a loss to myself as your letter by soliciting another. Since I wrote Christmas and New Years and all their concomitant joys have fled and we have been hurriedly launched into another year, before the close of which how many hopes now budding will be withered? How many fondly cherished schemes dashed into nothingness, and cheeks, now glowing with "the rose tint of health", paled by the icy touch of death. But pardon me for starting in your mind such a melancholy train of thought, though you will agree there are pleasures, real pleasures which cluster around a Christmas fire a home, and which you have no doubt tasted. All welcome the approach of that festal day, consecrated as it is by a time-honored custom to universal rejoicing, with emotions of delight (Turn to page 3) to the old folks its advent brings back many a cherished recollection of their young days; Youth looks forward to it with all the glorious anticipation with which the future is wont to delight fancy's eye; and even our Negroes ask with increased anxiety the number of weeks before Christmas, and cast many a lingering, longing look at Santa Claus vanishing in the distant past where he has unceremoniously hurled by the new year. I presume Christmas in Mississippi as well as her is a very different thing from Christmas in Virginia and you were no doubt forcibly struck with the contrast.

I have often wondered how you and Cousins Ann and Ruth amuse yourselves at Billy's Creek for if the mud is so prevalent you certainly cannot take your morning rambles and evening strolls which used to be your delight at Beaver Creek. My roommates lives at Tuscumbia, Alabama and from the accounts he receives from home I infer that the roads through that section are impassible {}, and therefore the mails must be extremely irregular.[176] Our winter has been extremely mild for this climate, at this season we generally have snow about two feet deep, but now there is scarcely any and to night the air is delightful and the moon shedding its full flood of light on mountain plain and river gives the whole the air of enchantment. I wish so much that you were here to share it with me.

Brother Alick paid me a very unexpected visit last month, which gave me much pleasure. He was complaining of the cold weather all the time and seemed to suffer so much from it that I could not prevail upon him to stay even a day. He brought from Sister Mary a nice plum cake, which was of course delicious. I fear however that the Cold has scared him so he will never be tempted to honor the Point with his presence again.

The flattering notice, which you bestowed on a rhyme, which I put at the bottom of the page in a former letter, has emboldened me to send in this another specimen which I indited a few days before Christmas, which may contribute to your amusement. If I succeed in that I will doubtless experience all the gratification of a real bard. But it is not without a considerable degree of distrust that I hazard such a performance to your perusal, lest the ridicule it may excite may even over-reach the liberal allowance which your goodness would otherwise

---

[176] James Deshler(1833-1863) a graduate of West Point served in the US and CS Army rising to the rank of brigadier general before losing his life at Chickamauga.

interpose in its behalf. To say that I do not feel a strong partiality for it would be to disown that parental devotion with which nature has endowed every creature for its offspring, but to expect of you a like blindness to it's faults would be far more than I can hope. You will at least give the sentiment it breathes the credit of sincerity, and I hope love not less the scenes and events it attempts to commemorate, scenes which stand in prominent and beautiful relief upon the tablet of the past.

If there ever was an individual anxious for a time to arrive I certainly am for next June. The nearer it approaches the more difficult do I find it to decide upon what business to adopt for life. At present I feel pretty sure of staying in the army of a while, and to make that while depend upon circumstances. How would you like to see your Cousin a Lawyer? It is a popular sentiment that (Turn to page 2) a good lawyer must be a great Liar, and consummate scoundrel but I trust you will never think the less of Cousin James for being a lawyer.

I spend every Saturday evening in the society of ladies of my acquaintance on the Point, in which I find great relief and pleasure after a week's study; no other time is allowed to us, we are even more restricted than the Negroes for they have till Monday morning. I have a bouquet now on the mantle, which was sent to me the other day by Mrs. Lee who as you are aware is my most particular friend among the ladies.[177] I can never say too much in her praise. Of Mrs. Berard's family I might with propriety say the same. One of the Miss Berards, who by the way has in some way heard of the gourd says she intends to make you a Rigulette {} to send by me next June; they are very fashionable here and I think very becoming. Won't you come on and get it? I hope you will excuse the

---

[177] At Cooleemee plantation there was once a twig of arbor vitae with an inscription in the handwriting of Columbia Stuart Hairston stating "From a boquet give James E. B. Stuart by Mrs. Lee of West Point." Probably at UNC-Chapel Hill after the death of Judge Peter Hairston.

trouble, which my carelessness has given you to keep the run of the pages, but as a soldier never ought to retreat I thought it would never do to begin on another sheet especially as my stock of paper is "growing smaller by degrees and beautifully less."

How do you manage about going to church in Mississippi? I think Professor Sprole preached one of the ablest sermons on New Years day I ever heard, I will miss his excellent sermons when I leave.[178] Unlike other Colleges, where the studies and duties become a mere trifle the last year, at West Point they are multiplied ten fold; we have a great deal to do and little time to do it in. We are now studying Permanent Fortifications, Thrioux' Treatise on Artillery (in French) and having just finished Kent's Commentarys on International law, we began Moral science yesterday, but I have no doubt this list is as uninteresting to you as it is to us.

Riding during cold weather is about all the exercise we take except skating. From the former we still derive great pleasure; in the Riding Hall we are exercised principally at cutting with our sabers at artificial heads, while going at full speed, with some heads on the ground and some about the height of a man. Some become so expert at this mock slaughter of heads, that I fear they would prove formidable antagonists in the field. Don Quixote I still consider the best among the horses, he goest through the exercise like a steak, but as he kicks up whenever my sabre scabbard strikes him behind I suppose that he won't "toat double" otherwise he is as graceful and chivalrous as the old Knight himself. As for the skating to those who know how, it is doubtless a splendid pastime but I have never learned for I have always had a sort of presentiment that my first essay on skates would cost me my neck. It is by no means an

---

[178] William T. Sprole was chaplain and professor of ethics and English studies from 1847 until 1856 at West Point.

uncommon thing for ladies to skate her north. I understand Miss Mary Lee has been making some preserving efforts in that line on a pond in her backyard.

Having I feared succeeded too well in tiring you this time I beg of you to write as soon as you get this and let me know what you are doing in Mississippi. Give my best love to all. Pa is now in Richmond.[179] John has given up his practice and has turned farmer in Drum Head.[180] All well in Virginia when last heard from.

                        I remain yours affectionately
                        J. E. B. Stuart

TO BETTIE HAIRSTON

    United States Military Academy, West Point, New York
    May 8, 1854

My Dear Cousin,

As I was the first one of your correspondents to welcome you in Mississippi, I will certainly not be the last to greet you with an Old Virginia welcome upon your arrival at Beaver Creek. The wide gap of several months in our correspondence has I know affected me more than any one else, for without any joke Cousin Bettie your letters always give me so much pleasure that were it not wishing you so much trouble I would wish for one every day. I received your last favor from Billy's Creek; just the day after having despaired of ever receiving it I wrote another to you. Yours had been on the road so long that I very much doubt whether mine ever reached you. Without any reflexion upon your adopted state I considered it perfectly useless to persevere in writing at

---

[179] Archibald Stuart was a Virginia State Senator from 1852 until 1854
[180] JEBS brother John Dabney Stuart returned to Laurel Hill to farm in Patrick County.

least until an answer from you would give evidence like the dove to Noah that the floods had subsided, and rendered mail communications practicable in Mississippi. But so far no such dove has arrived and I fear that she either never started or has been turned from her course and is perhaps at this very time perched in a corner of some uninviting P. O. This however is rather too figurative for such old heads as ours.

  Your paradise of a garden must be enchantingly lovely now, I can almost imagine that I see you just as you appeared two years ago with roses blooming around you while Woodbine fragrant honeysuckle and lovely japonica in sweet profusion surround you, and just as your blue eye had feasted itself on the beauties around you a humming bird rested his weary pinion on the very twig from which you had just plucked a rose and with its tiny eye cast an accusing look at you. This picture I hope soon to realize. I am confident that you never in your life walked with a more elastic tread, than when you promenaded those garden walks on your return of Virginia. Virginia is the place after all, isn't it? Mississippi may do for cotton but give me Virginia for comfort. I have been so long intending to send you a sketch of some of the scenes around here that I am really ashamed of myself for delaying it so long. Be assured however that I will send it in June. I send the music by this mail. They are pieces much admired as played by the band but I do not know how they will sound on the piano. They were copied for me by he leader of the Band, a German of high musical attainments, the only objection to his performance is his taste is not quite American enough for national music.[181] He utterly abhors Yankee Doodle, which alone would condemn him in the estimation of many; but I do believe that his touching execution of "Home Sweet Home" the night before the

---

[181] Augustus Apelles, German violinist and organist was bandmaster and music teacher at USMA from 1843 until 1872.

Graduates leave would bring tears from adamant. I wish so much you could hear it next June. You would do no doubt resolve that no temptation in future however luring could entice you away from Beaver Creek. I write to you my Dear Cousin many things about West Point and myself, which I fear savor too much of egotism, but to you I feel disposed always to express myself freely.

Tell Cousin Peter (Little) to be of good cheer for it is quite probable that he will yet come if not in June at least in September which if anything would be preferable for he would thus avoid all the drudgery of Camp, which is particularly harassing to a "Plebe". My reason for this message is that my young friend from our District who would otherwise keep the vacancy filled for two years more it is thought will leave in June; though the latter is "entre nous" I have written to Mr. Bocock (who has by the way treated me with marked kindness, without any acquaintance or claim upon him) apprizing him of the possibility of such an event, and informing him that when it occurred the appointment of a successor would be more advantageous to take effect in September than June. I wrote to Cousin P. while at the University but have never received an answer.

We have had fine riding during the winter and spring I wish I could take Don Quixote home with me, I am so delighted with him. Did you see the Yankee lady, that took Jack's eye on your way out, or your return.

Mrs. Lee of whom you have so often heard me speak so highly, has left us for a visit of some months to Arlington, Virginia; the residence of her father. She was like a mother to me and I miss her in proportion, but in compliance with her invitation I will stop at Arlington, Virginia on my way home. As for the time of my reaching Virginia it is impossible for me to say anything definite, but I am certain that Cousin

Above, my friend Judge Peter Hairston at his home, Cooleemee Plantation in Davie County, North Carolina. Below, artist Pat G. Woltz rendition of Laurel Hill, Patrick County, Virginia.

Bettie will be among the first Virginians to see me unless something extraordinary occurs. I thank you again for your invitation and will endeavor to surprise you in my early time of taking advantage of it. I must not forget to mention the gourd, which still hangs "on yonder hook". Several of my Classmates declare their intention to break it before June because they say I am so "awful particular about an old gourd" but I do not anticipate such a calamity, the loss to them would be too great.

Honorable Mr. Clemens of Wheeling has been appointed Visitor from Virginia instead of Pa as was expected.[182] Mr. Bocock says the reason was that our District very recently had one (Mr. Wicher, by General Taylor who did not accept), and there exists a regulation requiring every other District to be represented before our again has a visitor. How would you like to get the appointment next? Our former Instructor in Mathematics at this place Lieut[enant] Samuel Jones (now Capt[ain]) has put forward by his friends in Virginia, his native state, for the post of Professor of Math at the University, vacated by the death of Professor Courtenay who was also a graduate here.[183] He was such a favorite here with every body and so well qualified too, that upon receiving information of the efforts of his friends, and at the instance of several of my classmates. I endeavored to show our appreciation of his worth by an article in the Examiner, which you will find the first thing in the no for April 17th.[184] But don't tell any one the author, I have since thought it so presumptuous that I feel ashamed of myself at the idea of a Schoolboy recommending a Professor for the first College in the Union.

---

[182] Sherrard Clemens (1820-1881) a Democrat represented Virginia in the U.S. House of Representatives from 1852 to 1853 and 1857 to 1861.

[183] Samuel Jones, Jr. (1819-1887) graduated USMA in 1841 and served as a general in the Confederate army. Edward H. Courtenay graduated USMA in 1821, died on December 21, 1853, taught at USMA and the University of Virginia.

[184] The Richmond Examiner, edited by Robert W. Hughes, claimed to be the largest paper in the South.

But I have the consolation that I was in a good cause and said nothing but truth. I must say my {} appearance in public print has been rather discouraging. I suppose you heard what a trick John D. and Duke Tompkins served me in publishing a piece of my doggerel in the "Floyd Intelligencer";[185] if you have not I hope you never will. I never felt so outraged in my life. I had the consolation in this case to know that the circulation of that majestic sheet would be limited by 100 yards from the printing office. I don't think they will succeed in making me a "poet" "nolens volens" I will never perpetrate a rhyme after I leave the Academy. Witness Cousin Bettie. This letter is already to long. Do write now, and believe me yours truly and affectionately.

      Love to all.
      J. E. B. Stuart

TO MRS. CLAUDIUS BERARD
  Willard Hotel, Washington D. C.
  June 19, 1854
Dear Friend,

  I send you by this mail a likeness of "Beauty". You perceive I was looking my prettiest when it was taken and I was thinking about the inmates of the cottage. I formed a traveling acquaintance with Miss Edwards of Illinois between West Point and New York. We parted with regret. I stayed in New York City just three minutes by the watch; one minute longer would have kept me till Monday. Arlington, Virginia yesterday, delighted, home tomorrow; the Capitol of friends here today.

  You are at liberty to show this daguerreotype to our mutual friends, but beware of _____. Tell Miss Emily if she knew how much

---

[185] Floyd Intelligencer was the newspaper for Floyd County, Virginia. Research did not reveal a copy of Stuart's poem as only three issues are known to exist.

trouble hers gave me should say I deserved it. Placards were stuck up at numerous depots, etc. to "beware of pickpockets," and as the pressure from the crowd was very great I feared exceedingly that someone would feel it in my coat pocket, mistake it for a purse and hive it. To present such a catastrophe I had to keep my hand on it all the time. Excuse haste.

      Yours truly,
      J. E. B. Stuart

Love to <u>all</u>, au revoir.

TO PETER W. HAIRSTON
  Salem, North Carolina
  August 3, 1854

Dear Cousin P (eter)

  I came over this morning from Mr. Shepperd's having arrived there last evening from Mr. Williams'.[186] I left Cooleemee Hill Tuesday evening for Mr. Williams wishing to see my friends there once more before leaving the Country. Mr. Williams arrived yesterday morning to breakfast from Mocksville with news that Mr. Lillington was somewhat better but he is still considered in a very critical situation, though not in immediate danger, Drs. Swan of Salisbury and some body else are in almost constant attendance. Mr. Jacocks preached in Mocksville Sunday.[187] My sisters Mr. Smith and myself attended, dining at Mr. L's thence we returned to Cooleemee Hill with Mr.. Jacocks and Mr. Smith went to Mr. Williams from there he has since started north.

---

[186] Augustine Henry Shepperd represented Forsyth County, North Carolina in the U. S. House of Representatives. His home was located in present day Winston-Salem, North Carolina, near Vargrave and Waughtown streets. Nicholas Lanier Williams was a member of the North Carolina Council of State and trustee at the University of North Carolina. His home on Panther Creek near the Shallowford of the Yadkin River was called God's Hill.

[187] J. A. Lillington was an attorney that lived in Mocksville, North Carolina. Doctors Swann and A.M. Nesbitt of Water Street in Salisbury, North Carolina.

Mrs. Shepperd and suite including Pender left your house Saturday evening leaving us all quite blue. I sometimes think that the taste of classmates for each other's society particularly West Pointers is unequalled by the strongest attachment and what is more remarkable, it becomes more and more intense as time continues.[188] A thought, which makes me fear that out of the army, I will be miserably unhappy. But "nous verrons" and "sufficient unto the day is the evil thereof" are considerations of importance to me, not meaning to say that I am lulled in a quiet listless resignation to "whatever fate betides me" without an exertion to avoid it, if bad or secure it if good but I do feel an abiding confidence in the events of His ordering which makes me to some extent free from the usual solicitude.[189]

But more about home, I take pleasure in informing you that "all's right" at Cooleemee Hill. Your house is progressing rapidly the brick had risen more than half way up the second story window and doorframes. In fact from my observation I am a little apprehensive as also Mr. Smith that they were going too fast, that the quantity was disproportionate with the quality of the work for the interior joints of masonry were not carefully filled and as accurately adjusted as principles of civil Engineering require, though it may be in this case as in most others that the general practice is a great variance with the theory. Lummie requested me to say in my letter that the plantation was getting on very well, though she said it [with] a sigh as much as to say she felt uneasy about you. I kept her laughing as long as I stayed by making myself ridiculous in various ways, crossing swords with Mr. Jacocks, etc.

---

[188] William Dorsey Pender graduated USMA in 1854, married Fanny Shepperd in 1859, and served as a general in the Confederate army during the Civil War.
[189] Peter W. Hairston had lived in France and JEBS was quoting directly to him in French meaning ?nous verrons?

The day I left the mail arrived and I will tell you confidentially a very characteristic joke on the Reverend gentleman. In the morning he was so much better that he was continually exulting over it but he got hold of the newspapers and after reading of Lieut[enant] Paine at Jefferson Barracks after three hours illness, one of my anticipated companions next winter, all the time betraying symptoms of alarm he concluded he would lie down and before I left he was the sickest man you ever saw.[190] Of course I laughed heartily at him and if he let the papers alone I have no doubt that my laughing proved as curative as bread-pills did on similar occasion, with a similar patient.

I will return to Mr. Shepperds this evening and leave tomorrow for Patrick. My horse I am afraid will not prove as good as he promised though I will sell him as soon as I can without a sacrifice. My reasons for buying you know were of the most urgent kind. You may rely upon my being at Uncle Marshall's during Henry Court unless something extraordinary happens. John D. also attends as a witness in a civil case of somebody vs. Rice of Floyd C. H.[191]

Sammy came out wonderfully before I left. He seemed to rival me as master of ceremonies and excelled me in gallantry for he gathered a beautiful bouquet of rosebuds and presented them to Miss Fanny Shepperd as he knew his father would have done if he bad been present. Mr. William (Architect) made him a little wagon on which Sammy has been hauling all kinds of produce running it more Sunday than any other day.[192] He will do your waggoning cheap for he charges no freight. Lummy gave me a letter from Young Ruffin to you requesting me to

---

[190] Ferdinand Paine of Maine graduated USMA in 1848 and died June 23, 1854.
[191] Patrick, Henry and Floyd were counties in Virginia were members of the Stuart and Hairston families lived.
[192] Cooleemee was built by the firm of Conrad and Williams of Raleigh, North Carolina

give it to you at Henry Court.[193] She said it was expressive of some doubts as to the validity of the title to some land you intended buying near Sauratown and asking you to defer the bargain till you could confer together.[194] I will have the letter for you at Henry.

Give my best love to Uncle Marshall's family, and to such other of my relations as you may meet and to whom you may consider it acceptable. Tell Cousin Bettie I will be at Beaver Creek about the 15th and let me ask of you as a favor not to tease her about me. Miss Mary Joyner and Joe, but more this anon. My paper is out au revoir.

Very truly yours,
J. E. B. Stuart

PRAYER, September 10, 1854, Sunday

O God where'er my footsteps stray
Or prairies far or battles dim
Still keep them in thy holy way.
And cleanse my soul from ev'ry sin.

Lord! When the hour of death shall come
And from this clay my soul release
O grant that I may have a home
In they abode of endless peace.

---

[193] A son of Chief Justice Thomas Ruffin of North Carolina.
[194] Saura Town was a plantation located near the historic Native-American village of Upper Saura Town along the Dan River in Stokes County.

TO BETTIE HAIRSTON

American Hotel, Richmond, Virginia

September 27, 1854

Dear Cousin

I have at length learned something definite in regard to my ultimate destination but before touching upon the uninteresting details, I must recur to scenes to which I have often recurred with delight, and inquire after our friends in Dear Old Henry; having heard nothing to the contrary I presume that Uncle Marshall is entirely restored and that the gloom which hung over the hearts at Beaver Creek during his illness, has long since been dissipated by cheerful warmth of the family circle. On my way to Salem I found all your friends well and full on anxious inquiries about you; I endeavored to deliver all your messages to Cousins Lucreatia Hardaman and Cornelia.[195] If I failed, attribute to a treacherous memory but not to any indisposition to oblige you.

Salem, Virginia

September 29, 1854

I began this letter in Richmond but before concluding it I was taken sick and confined to my bed till this morning. Dr. Cabell's early attendance shortened an attack, which might have terminated differently.[196] I have not recovered my lost appetite a loss which I have so seldom been made to feel that it almost grieves me, especially when I find myself unable to do justice to a meal for which I have to pay full price, for it has always been my consolation that I always got the worth of my money in the eating line, and precious little did a hotel keeper ever make off me. I came up in the accommodation train from Lynchburg this evening that

---

[195] Lucretia Nash Hardeman married John Hardeman in 1862 and later married Thomas Hardeman.

[196] Dr. James Lawrence Cabell (1813-1889) taught medicine at the University of Virginia.

stops at this place where I will have to stay till tomorrow. But I must trouble [you] with an account of my adventures after returning speedily from Davie, via Salem (where who must I meet but Cousin P--) home. There I found the long looked-for document from Head Quarters awaiting my perusal; I found that I was in consummation of my wishes appointed a Second Lieut[enant] in the Mounted Rifles, a Corps which my taste, fondness for riding, and desire to serve my country in some acceptable manner led me to select above all the rest.[197] When I saw you I felt confident that my belonging to that Regiment would require me to spend some time at Jefferson Barracks but in this I was mistaken for the order I received required me to join my company in Texas, by the 15th of October. Upon a moment's reflection I liked this arrangement better than the former one; for the depredations of the Camanches on the Texan Frontier have given my regiment active service for some time, and I had much rather see active service at the start than to have it deferred.[198] I was assigned to the identical company commanded by Capt[ain] Van Buren when he was killed last July, now posted at Fort McIntosh Laredo Texas.[199] I accordingly left home the day after I saw these orders, to set out from Wytheville as soon as my letters were accredited, via New York to Texas. But on arriving in Washington to my surprise I found in an interview with the Adjutant General, that an order had been issued extending my leave until the 15th of October leaving me at least two weeks to stay at home. I however went on to New York equipped myself fully for Texas, spent a few days with Pete and am now on my way to take home folks by surprise.[200] I expect to remain closely at Patrick till

---

[197] A Regiment of Mounted Rifles was created in 1846.
[198] The Comanche tribe had become a problem to the settlers in west Texas.
[199] Michael E. Van Buren of Maryland and Michigan joined the Mounted Rifles in 1846 and died in 1854.
[200] The Cooleemee Plantation Papers show that Peter Hairston loaned JEBS $150 on July 21, 1854.

the 15th when I will take the quickest route to Texas. I can not say that it affords me much pleasure to be thus delayed, in only doubles the pain of parting and besides, I can not fancy this way of always going but never gone. But I believe it is for my own good I am persuaded that "all things are for the best" though we may not be conscious of it at the time. As regards my entering the army I may as well add that I have but one aim, and that is to do some service to my country in return for what she has done for me. I might it is true enter civil life with many advantages and there are manifold considerations in my case would make it very desirable, I might also nominally cancel my sense of duty to my country, by entering that portion of the service entirely unexposed to actual fighting, and thus spend my life in inglorious ease at some delightful station on the Atlantic but when there are hard knocks to be felt, and hard blows to be dealt, a man really desirous to serve his country will not hesitate a moment to declare for the latter. I beg pardon my Dear Cousin for talking to you so much about myself, but I really take so much interest in you all that I take it for granted, which perhaps I ought not to do, that you feel the same for me.

  Pete is coming on finely, I went to his room and found him busy unraveling the mysteries of Algebra. From all accounts he is studious, sober, military and much beliked by his companions. He has improved vastly by his new costume, but laughs as much as ever I fear that propensity has cost him some demerit for there is an old saying that a "Plebe" can find more than any one else to laugh at. Tell George I think Pete will never forgive him for disappointing him so by failing to go to the Point. I could have staid months at that delightful spot and then they would have seemed like hours. I was afraid however that my frequent visits to Pete might distract his attention from his studies. I feel no doubt about his success. Cadets entering now will have to remain five years before graduating. Pete just missed it. I saw Judge Jones on the cars to day, he looks finely and will be in Henry next week.

I intended telling you a few of my adventures, such as being taken for a horse drover in North Carolina and repeatedly bantered for a horse swap, asked if I belonged to Mr. –'s Circus, my being recognized at Saura town by my likeness to Lummie, all of which tended to relieve the monotony of the trip, also to cap the climax, on my presenting myself at the pay office in Washington how the clerk persisted that I was dead, and finally after I perseveringly protested that I was alive concluded that it was some other "Stuart", but we will I hope laugh over these some other time. Give my love to all our Henry Kin, particularly to the inmates of Beaver Creek. I have written you a good deal but not half what I could like to write. Write to me as soon as you can at Mount Airy, North Carolina and believe me Cousin,[201]

                                          Yours truly
                                          J. E. B. Stuart

---

[201] The Stuarts picked up their mail and attended church in Mount Airy, North Carolina, less than ten miles from the Laurel Hill Farm in Patrick County, Virginia. The future home of Andy Griffith is the future birthplace of the editor of this book.

"Bettie" Hairston as an older lady.

POEM: TO BETTIE

West Point, New York
December 24, 1854

The gentle night is drawing fast
Her sable curtain o'er
Old Hudson's calm unrufflect breast,
And Crow-nest's crown of snow;
Yet tho the night-winds softly sigh
And moonbeams round me play
I would that I had wings to fly
To Bettie—far way.

Blest spot my mem'ry clings to thee!
The spring where last we strayed!
How happy would my spirit be,
The woes of life allayed,
If on the banks of Beaver Creek,
I roamed the live-long day
To gather flow'rs and berries seek
With Bettie—far away.

The soldier's toils were ill-repaid
'Twere vain the foe to brave;
To draw the sword in Freedom's aid,
Or vict'rys boon to crave,
If in the battle's stirring din
And danger's dread array
No hope would spring a smile to win

From Bettie—far away.

The gourd that hangs on yonder hook
Once pressed my Bettie's lip
Her parting gift I ne'er forsook
But from it often sip
To Bettie's health; for dearer far,
Than vales where diamonds lay
Than heaven's brightest gleaming star
Is Bettie—far away.

That gourd I'll bear where'er I go
That name will be a charm
To nerve my arm 'gainst ev'ry foe
And ev'ry foe disarm.
'Mong those whom I can ne'er forget
(let none their worth gainsay)
I'll prize thee dearest-fondest yet
My Bettie—far away.

Peter Hairston, husband of Columbia L. Stuart, sister of J. E. B. Stuart. Hairston served on the staff of his cousins, Stuart and Jubal Early's staff during the Civil War

Index

A

Abingdon, 15
Aenead, 24
Alexander, 15, 18, 19, 21, 25, 31, 39, 42, 43, 57, 66, 85, 97
American Hotel, 125
Amherst County, 26
Apelles, 116
Arabella, 40
Ararat, Virginia, 2, 11, 12, 19, 137
Arbuckle, 60, 63
Averett, 28, 47, 48, 96
Ayres (Ayers), 17

B

Backus, 75
Baily, 16
Beaver Creek, 2, 70, 71, 77, 79, 82, 84, 90, 93, 96, 97, 98, 100, 104, 106, 108, 109, 112, 115, 117, 124, 125, 128, 130
Bell Tavern, 20
Benton, 29
Berard, 89, 95, 113
Berard, 120
Berry Hill, 45
Bingham, 40
Bliss, 40
Board of Visitors, 51, 64, 104
Bocock, 96, 117, 119
Bonaparte, 33
Boyd, 19, 23, 32, 68, 92, 96
Boyden, Nathaniel A., 17
Brady, 52, 53
Broadnax (Brodnax), 56, 106
Brown, 1, 3, 8, 15, 18, 34, 53, 61, 66, 84
Brown, Alexander Stuart, 15, 18, 19, 21, 25, 31, 39, 42, 43, 57, 66
James Ewell Brown
  Brown, James Ewell, 11, 55
Judge James Ewell Brown
  Brown, James Ewell Brown, 15, 16
Buchanan, 17, 64
Buckingham, 19, 20, 23

Byars, 22

C

Cabell, 26, 27, 37, 47, 60, 63, 83, 105, 125
Caesar, 19, 21
Calhoun, 33
Cameron, 106
Carr, 64
Carter, 72, 81, 97
Caskie, 69
Cass, 29, 64
Celia, 23
Chambliss, 50, 51
Charlottesville, 26, 32, 39, 58, 69
Chevalier, 26, 37, 67
Clay, 28, 33
Clemens, 29, 119
Clinton, 36
Cobbler Spring, 16
Comanche, 126
Cooleemee, 64, 85, 113, 121, 122, 123, 127
Coon, 23
Courtenay, 119
Crawford, 13, 25
Crawford, 25
Crockett, 18, 20, 21
Crow's Nest, 33, 89
Crystal Palace Exposition, 72
Cushing, 92
Custis, 95

D

Dabney, 15, 16, 20, 22, 23, 26, 61, 84, 107, 115
Dade, 37
Dan River, 124
Davis, 29, 98, 109
Davis, Jefferson, 28, 29, 98, 99
Dawne, 29
Deshler, 112
Dialectic Society, 33, 88, 101
Dickens, 58
Douglas, 12, 29, 64
Downs, 29

133

Draper Valley, 17, 18

E

Ellmore, 29
Emory and Henry College, 15, 22, 23

F

Fillmore, 28, 66, 92
Floyd, 16, 22, 48, 60, 66, 107, 120, 123
Floyd County, 16, 22, 60, 66, 107, 120
Fonthill, 73
Fort, James Edward, 99
Foster, 95
Frank, 99
Franklin Pierce
   Pierce, Franklin, 25, 28, 64, 79
Freeman, 12

G

Gaines, 31, 34, 35, 36, 45
Giles County, 72, 78
Gilmer, 69, 105
Gleaves, 20
God's Hill, 121
Goggin, 64, 66
Gordon, 20, 64
Graham, 2, 18

H

Hairston, 2, 13, 14, 34, 37, 47, 56, 60, 64, 68, 70, 75, 82, 83, 85, 92, 98, 105, 106, 109, 113, 122, 123, 127, 132
Hairston, Elizabeth "Bettie", 2, 13, 14, 34, 70, 71, 75, 77, 80, 81, 83, 84, 88, 90, 98, 100, 102, 104, 105, 106, 107, 110, 115, 119, 120, 124, 130, 131
Hardaman (Hardeman), 125
Harden, 37, 47, 61
Hardyman, 83
Headen, 22, 50, 52, 60, 66, 92, 106
Henry, 2, 11, 13, 15, 22, 23, 28, 33, 43, 47, 50, 59, 61, 64, 70, 72, 75, 82, 83, 104, 109, 121, 123, 124, 125, 128, 138, 140
Houston, 29

Howard, 101
Hughes, 119
Hunt, 53

I

Irving House, 25

J

Jacocks, 121, 122
Jefferson Barracks, 47, 123, 126
Jefferson, Thomas, 26, 27
Johnson, 58

K

Kansas, 11
Kent, 20, 23, 114
Koscuisko, 36
Kossuth, 57, 59

L

Laurel Hill, 11, 12, 15, 19, 22, 23, 115, 128, 137, 139
Lee, 11, 15, 16, 64, 91, 95, 100, 103, 113, 115, 117
Lee, Mary, 103
Letcher, 11, 13, 16, 29, 38, 93
Levi, 27
Levy, 27
Lillington, 121
Love Not, 80, 99
Lowndes County, 105
Lynchburg, 26, 61, 84, 125

M

Marrowbone, 83
Martinsville, 2, 70
McClellan, 14, 110
McKee, 18
Miller, 20, 22
Mocksville, 121
Montgomery, 93
Morpheus, 58
Mosby, 5
Mount Airy, 2, 128, 139

Mounted Rifles, 11, 126

N

Napoleon, 33, 42, 59
Nesbitt, 121
New York, 8, 11, 14, 28, 31, 32, 34, 35, 39, 40, 42, 43, 45, 47, 50, 51, 52, 53, 57, 58, 62, 66, 67, 68, 70, 72, 73, 77, 80, 81, 85, 88, 91, 92, 97, 98, 102, 105, 110, 115, 120, 126, 130

O

Omohundro, 40
Ovid, 24

P

George Whitfield Painter
  Painter, George W., 17
Painter, 17, 21, 28
Pannill, 11, 13, 16, 37, 38, 86
Panther Creek, 121
Patrick County, 2, 11, 17, 19, 22, 25, 139
Pegram, 26, 54, 56, 61, 64, 68, 69, 92, 95, 103, 104
Peirce, 20
Pender, 122
Pepper's Ferry, 16
Perry, 2, 3, 11, 137, 138, 139, 140
Perryville, 59
Phillips, 56
Pocahontas, 83
Poe, 60
Polk, 33
Pulaski, 11, 17
Pulaski County, 17
Putnam, 37, 74

R

Rayner, 105
Rice, 123
Richardson, 20
Richmond Examiner, 91, 119
Ringgold, 97
Roanoke, 19, 68, 69
Robertson, 7, 138, 140

Rogers, 40
Ruffin, 106, 123, 124

S

Sackett, 102
Salem, 26, 85, 88, 91, 92, 96, 97, 99, 102, 121, 125, 126
Saltville, Virginia, 17
Sanders, 27, 39
Santa Claus, 111
Saura Town, 124
Scott, 35, 53, 57, 72, 79, 106
Secretary of War, 25, 28
Shakespeare, 43, 108
Shepperd, 121, 122, 123
Shepperds, 123
Smyth, 23, 40
Southwest Virginia, 3, 9, 11, 15, 138
Sprole, 114
Stoneman, 49, 140
Stovall, 37, 82
Stuart, 139
Alexander Hugh Holmes Stuart
  Stuart, Alexander Hugh Holmes, 13, 41, 68
Stuart, Anne Dabney, 15, 20, 84
Stuart, Archibald, 13, 16, 25, 28, 30, 49, 55, 60, 65, 68, 84, 115
Stuart, Columbia Lafayette, 17, 19, 22, 33, 47, 60, 101, 113
Stuart, Elizabeth Letcher Pannill, 16, 68
Stuart, James Ewell Brown, 2, 8, 11,12, 15, 16, 17, 19, 20, 21, 22, 23, 25, 26, 29, 34, 37, 42, 48, 57, 62, 64, 70, 75, 80, 85, 86, 97, 98, 105, 110,113, 115, 120, 121, 124
Stuart, John Dabney, 16, 22, 23, 107, 115
Stuart, Mary Carter, 72
Stuart, Mary Tucker, 17, 22, 81
Stuart, Victoria Augusta, 17, 88
Stuart, William Alexander, 22, 23, 42, 112, 17, 20, 30, 34, 52, 70
Sukey, 15
Swann, 121

T

Taylor, 27, 28, 31, 72, 81, 119

Terrill, 59
Texas, 11, 29, 40, 60, 126
Tompkins, 120
Tyler, 27, 83

U

United States Military Academy, 8, 11, 14, 28, 31, 34, 39, 42, 43, 45, 50, 51, 57, 58, 62, 66, 67, 68, 70, 77, 81, 92, 97, 102, 105, 110, 115
University of North Carolina at Chapel Hill, 14, 56, 113
University of Virginia, 26, 27, 32, 39, 119, 125

V

Van Buren, 47, 126
Vermont, 82
Virginia Tech, 140

W

Walker, 29

Walton, 23
War Department, 51, 52
Webster, 28, 40
West Point, 8, 11, 13, 14, 28, 31, 33, 34, 35, 36, 37, 39, 42, 43, 45, 46, 50, 51, 52, 53, 57, 58, 59, 61, 62, 66, 67, 68, 70, 72, 73, 74, 77, 79, 81, 84, 85, 86, 88, 90, 91, 92, 93, 96, 97, 98, 102, 105, 106, 107, 110, 112, 113, 114, 115, 117, 120, 130
Wilcox, 109
Williams, 121, 123
Willis, 2, 35
Wise, 22
Witcher, 27
Wythe, 11, 15, 16, 17, 18, 19, 20, 22, 23, 28, 39, 48, 51, 58, 69, 84
Wytheville, Virginia, 15, 17, 19, 20, 21, 26, 60, 61, 68, 69, 70, 126

Y

Yalobusha River, 105
Yost, 23
Young, 19, 20, 29, 63, 123

About the Author

J. E. B. Stuart's biographer, Emory Thomas, describes Tom Perry as "a fine and generous gentleman who grew up near Laurel Hill, where Stuart grew up, has founded J. E. B. Stuart Birthplace, and attracted considerable interest in the preservation of Laurel Hill. He has started a symposium series about aspects of Stuart's life to sustain interest in Stuart beyond Ararat, Virginia." Perry graduated from Patrick County High School in 1979 and Virginia Tech in 1983 with a Bachelor's Degree in history.

Tom founded the J. E. B. Stuart Birthplace in 1990. The non-profit organization has preserved 75 acres of the Stuart property including the house site where J. E. B. Stuart was born on February 6, 1833. Perry wrote the eight interpretive signs about Laurel Hill's history along with the Virginia Civil War Trails sign and the new Virginia Historical Highway Marker in 2002. He spent many years researching and traveling all over the nation to find Stuart materials. He continues his work to preserve Stuart's Birthplace, producing the Laurel Hill Teacher's Guide for educators and the Laurel Hill Reference Guide for groups.

Perry can be seen on Virginia Public Television's Forgotten Battlefields: The Civil War in Southwest Virginia, with his mentor noted Civil War Historian Dr. James I. Robertson, Jr. Perry has begun a collection of papers relating to Stuart and Patrick County history in the Special Collections Department of the Carol M. Newman Library at Virginia Tech under the auspices of the Virginia Center for Civil War Studies.

He is the author of over ten books on Patrick County, Virginia, including Ascent to Glory, The Genealogy of J. E. B. Stuart, The Free State of Patrick: Patrick County Virginia in the Civil War, J. E. B. Stuart's Birthplace: The Dear Old Hills of Patrick: J. E. B. Stuart and Patrick County, Virginia, Images of America: Patrick County Virginia, Images of Henry County Virginia, and Notes From The Free State Of Patrick.

Historian Tom Perry at the site he saved, J. E. B. Stuart's Birthplace, the Laurel Hill Farm, just outside Mount Airy in Patrick County, Virginia.

In 2004, Perry began The Free State of Patrick Internet History Group, which has become the largest historical organization in the area, with over 500 members. It covers Patrick County, Virginia, and regional history. Tom produces a monthly email newsletter about regional history entitled Notes From The Free State of Patrick that comes from his website, www.freestateofpatrick.com.

Historian Thomas D. Perry is the author and publisher of over forty books on regional history in Virginia surrounding his home county of Patrick. A Virginia Tech graduate, he studied under renowned Civil War Historian, James I. "Bud" Robertson, and speaks all over the region and country. Perry's collection of papers, books, and images are housed in the Special Collection Department of the Carol M. Newman Library at Virginia Tech.

In 2009, Perry used his book Images of America Henry County Virginia to raise over $25,000 for the Bassett Historical Center, "The Best Little Library in Virginia," and as editor of the Henry County Heritage Book raised another $30,000. Perry was responsible for over $200,000 of the $800,000 raised to expand the regional history library.

He is the recipient of the John E. Divine Award from the Civil War Education Association, the Hester Jackson Award from the Surry County Civil War Round Table, and the Best Article Award from the Society of North Carolina Historians for his article on Stoneman's Raid in 2008. In 2010, he received acknowledgement from the Bassett Public Library Association for his work to expand the Bassett Historical Center and was named Henry County Virginia Man of the Year by www.myhenrycounty.com. Perry also recently received the National Society of the Daughters of the American Revolution Community Service Award from the Patrick Henry Daughters of the American Revolution.

Books on J. E. B. Stuart by Thomas D. Perry

Visit  for more information

Made in the USA
Middletown, DE
24 March 2023